UNEXPLORED
PARIS

With special thanks to:

Daniel Catan,

Alexandre Gady,

Anne-Marie Joly, Notre-Dame Museum Curator,

Pierre-Émile Renard,

Danièle Rousseau-Aicardi,

Pierre Cavillon,

Pierre Housieaux, of the Association for the Preservation and Enhancement of Historical Paris,

Paul Bonno, directeur of the Wine Museum,

Georges-Olivier Châteaureynaud, general secretary of the Literary Society and Cristina Campodonico, public relations officer,

M. Roland-Gosselin, chairman of the Charity Bazaar Memorial,

including the Paris-Nature Section of the City of Paris Parks, Gardens and Green Space Department,

the staff at Montmartre Museum,

and all those who gave us friendly advice and support during these long walks.

Front cover (left to right, top to bottom):
Saint-Séraphin Church (15th), Romantics Museum (9th), Hameau Boileau (16th), turncock's house (14th), Cité Verte (14th), Cour de l'Étoile-d'Or (11th), Rue des Fêtes (19th), Cour du Coq (11th), Villa Adrienne (14th).

Back cover (top to bottom):
Impasse Marie-Blanche (18th), stairway outside the turncock's house (14th), Saint-Vincent Nature Garden(18th), houses in Rue Cassini (14th).

You will find the contents on pp. 186-189.

Rodolphe Trouilleux

UNEXPLORED
PARIS

Photographs by Jacques Lebar

Translated by Patricia Abbou

Parigramme

Nectar in the streets of Paris

Unexplored Paris... France's capital still has some surprises in store for many of its visitors, already familiar with the more renowned historical landmarks of the city. Unexplored side streets, courtyards and cul-de-sacs can tell stories about momentous historical events as well as ordinary, day-to-day life of bygone days, and this book will serve as a guide to those "uncharted monuments", hidden away in unexpected places. However, as any explorer knows, such treasure troves can only be chanced upon by strolling along the city streets, taking time to "stand and stare", and even running the risk of getting lost.

The rewards will be manifold: secluded, leafy cul-de-sacs, cobblestoned courtyards, homes of poets and painters, elegant buildings, and, believe it or not, "villages" nestling in the heart of Paris, all of which can be likened to golden threads running through the very fabric of the city's history. Guidebooks often point out that it is worth taking time out from the usual tourist haunts to go and visit a particular site they wish to highlight. In Paris, however, such advice is practically superfluous, as these lesser known sites are almost all in close proximity to the more well-known ones. Taking time out in this case is more a question of deciding whether to make a short detour, or turn down one street in preference to another, just for the pleasure of making a discovery. A fleeting glimpse of an unusual building, a secluded garden, a picturesque view, through a half-open door or down a side street, is usually enough to whet the appetite!

The delight taken in building up a personal museum collection of historic relics depends on two factors: an open mind and a passion for history in all its forms. Strollers, whose curiosity is aroused and who allow themselves to be guided by their whims and temperament, will collect their finds like bees gathering nectar. They will come upon secluded cul-de-sacs, cloisters, manor houses, artists' ateliers, inscriptions of all sorts, greenery, old shop signs, all with one thing in common: the incalculable power to enchant lovers of Paris wishing to become more intimately acquainted with the city's history.

Our aim has been to compile a book supplying information on sites hardly ever mentioned in tourist guides, and to which access is fairly easy. However, we have had to leave out many charming spots, which are under lock and key and are not on view to the general public. The list is neither exhaustive nor final. On the contrary, the contents often fluctuate owing to the constantly changing face of Paris, and, unfortunately, fine specimens are frequently "struck" off the list. Nevertheless, we are all free to contribute our own precious discoveries to this catalogue of fragile relics.

Straying from the beaten track and looking at Paris from another angle, as one might scrutinize the reverse side of a garment to see how it is made, is a delightful way of becoming even better acquainted with the city, but on certain conditions. "Fragile, handle with care!" is the password. The appeal of these sites stems mainly from the fact that they are readily accessible and "unmapped". This means, of course, that each one of us is, to a certain extent, responsible for their upkeep, and care must be taken not to upset the already precarious equilibrium of the capital city's "endangered species" – precious, often unprotected, relics of the city's past.

Visitors interested in history do not, of course, set out to despoil the city landscape, but, on the contrary, constantly bear witness to it, and, if necessary, protect it. For this, they will be richly rewarded, as they will have the infinite joy of taking home the nectar they have gathered down previously unexplored alleys and courtyards of Paris, and transforming it into honey by sharing it with their families and friends.

An ox "all dolled up" in grandma's clothes!

THE FORMER BŒUF À LA MODE RESTAURANT, 8 RUE DE VALOIS
Métro: Palais-Royal

While the "Grand Véfour" is the most well-known old restaurant in the Palais-Royal area, the "Bœuf à la Mode" must be the most unheard of; customers used to flock there, but all that remains today are the façade and the sign.

The restaurant was first called "Méot" when it opened in 1796, and then "Bœuf à la Mode" (Fashion-conscious Ox). It got its name both from the sign representing an ox and from a statuette in the dining area. The latter's style of dress depended on Paris fashions in vogue at the time. During the French Directory, government of the First Republic of France (1795-99), a certain Mr Tissot dressed the ox up as a *Directoire* dandy. During the Restoration of the Bourbons (1830), it wore a dress and shawl, complete with feathered hat and pendant earrings.

Good, plain cooking was served in the small dining room, and there were reception and private dining rooms on the mezzanine below. However, the restaurant went out of fashion, and ended up as a small bar. It had several owners, including the famous Prosper Montagné, before closing down in 1936. A gallery specializing in animal art was opened there recently.

The rather inconspicuous sign is still there, hardly ever noticed by those walking past. And yet, what could be more eye-catching than an ox "all dolled up" in grandma's clothes!

The astrologer's tower

COLONNE MÉDICIS
RUE DE VIARMES
Métro: Châtelet or Louvre. Not open to the public.

Right next to the Bourse de Commerce stands a tall column which looks somewhat out of place here. It is one of the monuments of Paris most surrounded by mystery. At the bottom, there is an inscription in latin stating that it is the sole relic of the manor house built by Catherine de Médicis (Queen of France, wife of Henry II) on the site of one of Louis d'Orléans' residences in 1572. She had the 31-metre-high tower built for her astrologer, Cosimo Ruggieri, who had considerable influence over her. This "handsome, sombre-looking man, who had a way with instruments, sometimes clad in trunk hose, always dressed in black", often used to climb to a chamber at the top of the tower with his patron, in order to mutter magic formulae and read the future in the stars.

A spiral staircase of 147 steps leads up to this chamber whose walls used to be made entirely of glass. All that remains is a metal skeleton, buffeted by the wind. Nobody knows what the building was used for, although the cardinal points are marked on the corners of the capital of the tower.

After Ruggieri's death in 1615, the column fell into disuse. The manor house became a shabby gambling establishment where card games such

as lansquenet were played, and, in 1748, was demolished in order to settle the debts of its last owner, Amédée de Savoie. The column narrowly escaped demolition and, in 1750, was sold to the Paris City Council who installed a fountain – run dry today – and a sundial.

In view of the upheavals that this district has gone through over time, the tower would appear to be protected by some sort of magic spell. Legend has it that on stormy nights, streaks of lightning reveal a tall, black silhouette in the metal cage at the top.

Recycled relics

SAINTE-AGNÈS CRYPT (AT THE EAST END OF SAINT-EUSTACHE CHURCH)
RUE MONTMARTRE
Métro: Les Halles

A small door topped with a shield indicates the entrance to the Sainte-Agnès crypt, at the east end of Saint-Eustache Church. The shield shows a fish about to bite its tail, a reminder that a man once made a fortune, thanks to the fish trade.

Jean Allais, citizen of 13th-century Paris, was the leader of the mystery play actors. He was also a creditor of Philip Augustus, Capetian King of France, and, as the latter was about to embark on the Third Crusade with Richard I of England, he requested compensation in the form of one *denier* per basket of fish sold at Les Halles. He quickly became rich, and, feeling a little guilty about it, had a chapel built for the merchants, dedicated to Saint Agnès. Over the centuries, it was extended, partly demolished, and then knocked down in the 16th century to make way for the church (dedicated to Saint Eustache) as we know it today – still unfinished.

The former chapel's basement gradually fell into disrepair, and was converted into a warehouse, as were a number of cellars nearby. About twenty years ago, it was used as a banana-ripening room. Out of curiosity, a priest had the place cleaned, and discovered a wall made out of stonework from previous chapels – capitals and other parts of columns – dating back to the 12th, 13th and 14th centuries. Regular exhibitions and discussions are held in the Sainte-Agnès crypt, and they will enable you to learn more about the relics of the chapel.

Bang!

PALAIS-ROYAL GARDENS
CENTRE LAWN OF THE GARDENS, AFTER THE BUREN COLUMNS
Métro: Palais-Royal

I n 1786, a certain Mr Rousseau, anxious to replace a sundial in Rue des Bons-Enfants, installed a small cannon in Palais-Royal gardens, perfectly aligned with the Paris meridian. The cannon would boom at midday precisely, thanks to an ingenious device whereby a magnifying glass converged on the cannon's fuse.

A few years ago, the custom was revived but with a difference – the human hand has taken over from optics, and a park keeper fires the cannon every day.

In the days when trade under the Palais-Royal arcades had more to do with the pleasures of the flesh than it does now, 18th-century poet Jacques Delille, known as Abbot Delille, wrote: *"Fields, meadows, woods, and flowers do not grace this garden. But while we are there and do wrong, We can also put our watches right."*

A reminder of world poverty

SAINT-GERMAIN-L'AUXERROIS CHURCH
PLACE DU LOUVRE
Métro: Louvre

Not many people know that, to the left of Saint-Germain-l'Auxerrois Church, there is a collection of mythical, medieval animals carved in stone. In order to see them, go into the courtyard located between the town hall and the church, behind the incongruous-looking bell-tower marking the dividing line between republic and religion, and look up towards the gargoyles. Underneath you will see some very strange representations of animals. The most unusual of these – a multitude of rats gnawing away at a globe – can be seen under the middle gargoyle, right next to a scene of suckling animals.

The sculptor's intention was to represent the world (the globe) gradually being destroyed by poverty (the rats), perhaps to remind passers-by of the harsh realities of life...

There are another two such sculptures in France, one on Le Mans Cathedral and the other on Saint-Siffrein-de-Carpentras Church, but with one notable difference: the rats here are gnawing their way in, whereas in Paris they are gnawing their way out.

On close inspection, just above the rats, you can see a rather diabolical figure of a cat watching the rodents at work.

Charnel houses and small shops

THE FORMER INNOCENTS CEMETERY
RUE DES INNOCENTS/RUE DE LA FERRONNERIE
Métro: Les Halles

Between the 12th and 18th centuries, Square des Innocents used to be the site of the biggest cemetery in Paris. When Innocents Cemetery was demolished in 1780, more than two million people had been buried in the communal graves! This was due to the fact that parishes without cemeteries, including the morgue and Hôtel-Dieu hospital, also buried their dead there. The cemetery became overcrowded, and to make room for more graves, charnel houses in the form of arcades were built around it, and bones disinterred and deposited under the roofs. This did not deter those still in the land of the living! Small shops, public letter-writers, prostitutes, and crooks all prospered under the arcades. Despite this bustling activity, the charnel houses were destroyed during the second half of the 18th century. In 1786, the bones from the cemetery were transferred to disused quarries, which later became the Denfert-Rochereau Catacombs.

There are no signs of these charnel houses today. The present building has arcades and shops, thus continuing the pursuits of centuries ago, albeit in less macabre surroundings than those of the *Ancient Régime* (social and political system before the French Revolution)!

The passageway through the building in Rue des Innocents leads to Rue de la Ferronnerie. There are marks on the ground to indicate where King Henry IV's carriage stood on May 14th, 1610, the day Ravaillac, a religious fanatic, plunged his knife into the heart of the King of France (who had obtained toleration for the Huguenots with the Edict of Nantes in 1598).

Signs of Old Paris

RUE MONTORGUEIL
Métro: Les Halles or Sentier

Some of the shop signs, still on view today, bear witness to the thriving trades of the past.

At no. 9, near Saint-Eustache Church, there is the "Au Croissant" sign of the cabaret with its crescent moon pointing its tips to the sky.

At no. 38, on the other side of the street, stands the "Escargot d'Or" (Golden Snail), one of the oldest restaurants in Paris, founded in 1832. The painted ceiling in the entrance hall was taken from actress Sarah Bernhardt's manor house, and is visible from the street. A brief foray into Rue Tiquetonne on your right, after crossing Rue Étienne-Marcel, is a must in order to admire the 18th-century "A l'arbre-à-liège" (Cork Oak) sign at no. 10.

The architect's tools in the fanlight at 51 Rue Montorgueil advertise the profession of Rohault de Fleury, who built the greenhouses in Jardin des Plantes in 1830. The renowned confectioner's, Stohrer, with its wall paintings under glass, is just nearby.

B etween the 13th and 19th centuries, wholesale fish merchants from the ports of Normandy, delivering fish and oysters to Les Halles, went down Rue Montorgueil every day. Owing to the intense activity of the huge market nearby, this street was, and still is, very busy, with its many taverns, inns and shops.

At no. 78, where Rue Greneta joins Rue Montorgueil, "Le Rocher de Cancale" (Cancale Rock), founded in 1820, has a sign in the form of a cast-iron rock with oysters clinging to it. It was also a tailor's shop for a long time before becoming a restaurant again.

Place du Caire and its big nose

PASSAGE DU CAIRE
237-39 RUE SAINT-DENIS/2 PLACE DU CAIRE
Métro: Réaumur-Sébastopol

Passage du Caire, just off Rue Saint-Denis, is the longest alley in Paris, and the result of a vast building operation carried out on land belonging to the Filles-Dieu Convent. In 1798, the company in charge called the new district, "The Cairo Fair", as Napoleon Bonaparte, future Emperor of France, was about to embark on his Egyptian Campaign.

Deliberate efforts were made to keep the decoration simple and the rents moderate; the latter encouraged people to set up business at very little cost. However, opinions on this differed greatly, as shown by Amédée de Kermel's comment in his book entitled *Le Livre des Cent et Un* (The Hundred and One Book), published in 1831: "I can see nothing of the treasures of Egypt, its perfumes, its children, the magnificence of its monuments. Cairo in this corridor! Sacrilege, sheer sacrilege!"

Egypt's splendour is more clearly evoked by the building in Place du Caire, a pastiche of Egyptian and neogothic styles. If you look carefully, you will see a strange profile, with an enormous nose, in the cornice. It is the portrait of Bouginier, a painter who often visited the atelier run by Antoine Gros (former pupil of David and Napoleon Bonaparte's official painter), and whose extraordinary nose was often caricatured by his friends on the walls of Paris.

Rococo house
narrowly escapes Haussmann's plans

HÔTEL DE SAINT-CHAUMOND, 226 RUE SAINT-DENIS/131 BOULEVARD DE SÉBASTOPOL
Métro: Strasbourg-Saint-Denis

Manor house façade overlooking
Boulevard de Sébastopol, with Rue
Saint-Denis in the background.

The porch at 226 Rue Saint-Denis opens into an unevenly paved courtyard, which reveals a fine, freestone façade at the far end.

This manor house (another storey has been added) was built by Jacques Hardouin-Mansart in 1734 at the request of the Saint-Chaumond nuns at no. 224. They wished to put up some of their wealthier residents there, usually women involved in separation procedures. The French Revolution proved fatal for the convent, and its chapel was closed. A certain Mr Michelet set up his printer's shop there, and his son, Jules, later acclaimed as one of France's leading historians, was born there.

An escutcheon, flanked by two consoles supporting a splendid, wrought-iron balcony, crowns the main entrance to the manor house. A passage through the building leads to another courtyard where a second, more graceful-looking façade, along with a work by Nicolas Pineau, portraying the delicate features of a woman's face, may be admired.

Another passage through a late 19th-century building leads from this courtyard to 131 Boulevard de Sébastopol.

As you can see, sometimes just an entrance is all that separates the winding streets of 18th-century Paris from the straight, austere boulevards designed by Haussmann (under Napoleon III he demolished older parts of Paris and replaced them with long, wide avenues).

The photographer who saw red

THE FORMER STUDIOS OF NADAR THE PHOTOGRAPHER
35 BOULEVARD DES CAPUCINES
Métro: Opéra

During the Second Empire when Napoleon III ruled as emperor, many photographers such as Disderi, Bisson, Le Gray, Mayer, to name but a few, set up business along the busy Grands Boulevards where clients were legion. Félix Tournachon, known as Nadar, was one such photographer who, already very experienced, opened his studio at 35 Boulevard des Capucines in 1860.

The building had only one storey, and Nadar converted it into a veritable glass palace with the help of new metal construction work technology. His most recent photographic works were presented in the shop on the ground floor; the first floor had luxuriously-appointed reception rooms, while the second housed his studio, air-conditioned by means of water continuously flowing down the glass walls. Everything was painted in red – the photographer had an obsession for red – and he always wore a crimson frock coat.

Nadar was the first to install a neon sign – on the balcony and still there today – made by a craftsman called Antoine Lumière, a name of the future, as, some years later, he presented his sons' invention, a motion-picture camera, at the "Grand Café" on the other side of the boulevard.

In 1872, Nadar left Boulevard des Capucines for less ostentatious premises in Rue d'Anjou because of debts incurred by his passion for aerostation.

In 1993, promoters demolished Nadar's studios, showing total disregard for its distinguished past. However, they did spare the glass façade and the front door.

A prison tower for safety

JEAN SANS PEUR TOWER
20 RUE ÉTIENNE-MARCEL
Métro: Étienne-Marcel

Jean sans Peur Tower is a rare example of architectural design in feudal times in Paris. In the early 15th century, Jean sans Peur, the Duke of Burgundy, inherited Hôtel d'Artois, on the site of Philip Augustus' enclosure. He shut himself away there after he had had Louis d'Orléans (brother of Charles VI, known as Charles the Foolish, whose daughter Catherine of Valois married Henry V of England) assassinated on November 23rd, 1407, thus starting a civil war between the Armagnac and Burgundy factions. Fearing revenge from the Armagnac faction, he built a fortified, rectangular tower, 23 metres high, onto the house. At the top were two high-security chambers, one above the other. This closely guarded residence was protected by machicolations, still there today, and crenellations. An empty, 10-foot-high chamber was built under the two security chambers, to prevent assault and any attempts to set fire to the floorboards. Double-locked metal gates and guards completed the defence system. The tympanum over the front door bears Jean sans Peur's coat of arms, a level crossed with a plumbline. A plane at each end of the level symbolizes the harm to be done to the bludgeon, emblem of Louis d'Orléans.

A medley of inscriptions

2 RUE DU MAIL
Métro: Bourse

History engraved in and painted on stone.

A police regulation dated July 30th, 1729 stipulated that street names be engraved on the walls of buildings at street corners. Inscriptions "MAI(L)" and "(R)UE VID(E) G(O)USSE(T)", still legible on the building on the corner of Rue du Mail and Rue Vide-Gousset, date from that time.

Just below, painted on the stone, are two inscriptions, very rare signs of the French Revolution in Paris: "SON DU MAIL" and "GM(E) (T)ELL". These few letters remind passers-by of the "Section du Mail", formerly "Section de la Place Louis XIV", which, in 1793, was to become "Section Guillaume Tell". Further down still are words, painted in black, partly obliterated and very difficult to decipher, prohibiting hackney carriages from stopping in the street ("aux voitures de place de s'arrêter dans cette rue").

Whether they be administrative, draw attention to revolutionary times, or vainly attempt to avoid the inevitable, these miscellaneous inscriptions have perhaps one thing in common: the power to stir your emotions as you discover fragile relics of the history of Paris.

The Vidocq staircase

GALERIE VIVIENNE
4 RUE DES PETITS-CHAMPS/6 RUE VIVIENNE
Métro: Bourse

the arcade which was first named after the notary, and then called Galerie Vivienne two years later. Its elegant features were one of the reasons for its instant success. Another was its proximity to Palais-Royal, a very busy district until Louis Philippe, known as the Citizen King, became established there. His "cleaning up" of the area led to its depopulation, and to that of the arcade.

At no. 13, there is staircase, with a wrought-iron balustrade, which the famous François Vidocq, former convict who became founder and head of a crime squad, used to climb. While he lived here in 1840, he set up a private police force for the protection of shopkeepers. He also defended many artists and writers, including personalities such as Victor Hugo and actress Juliette Drouet. Friend of Alexandre Dumas, the adventurer was described by Balzac, an expert on human nature, as a "great saver of souls".

In 1823, on the site of three manor houses, notary public Marchoux had architect F. J. Delannoy build

Beneath the ramparts of Charles V

PASSAGE SAINTE-FOY
AND RUES SAINTE-FOY, D'ABOUKIR AND DE CLÉRY
Métro: Strasbourg-Saint-Denis

In the mid-14th century, the city wall was extended to include the urban development spilling over the ramparts built by Philip Augustus, ramparts which in any case no longer offered much resistance to the new instruments of warfare. Charles V, King of France, known as Charles the Wise, had the new wall built on the right bank, in a curve from the Bastille, along the Grands Boulevards, up to Porte Saint-Denis, and, finally, back down to the Seine via Place des Victoires. The imposing fortification, 4,875 metres long, had a curtain wall 13 metres high, fronted by two ditches. The bigger one, 30 metres wide and 8 metres deep, was right next to the wall, and filled with water.

Before it was demolished in 1634, and its ditches filled in, the wall protected a population of up to 275,000. Today, there is nothing left except a few areas of uneven ground.

The narrow Passage Sainte-Foy, starting at 236 Rue Saint-Denis (you have to imagine that this was inside the city walls at that time), is not much to look at. At the end of the passage, if you go up the steep steps bringing it level with Rue Sainte-Foy, you will have climbed up onto the rampart's covered way.

In fact, Rue Sainte-Foy used to be called Rue du Rempart. Walk a few yards down Rue Sainte-Foy on the right-hand side as far as Rue Chénier, which will then take you straight to Rue d'Aboukir and Rue de Cléry, both parallel with one another. You are now outside the city wall. Rue d'Aboukir was built on the embankment of the big ditch when the rampart was demolished, and Rue de Cléry follows the former path along the counterscarp, the covered way outside the enclosure.

As you can see, a short stroll is all that is required in the 20th century to walk through a wall, cross a ditch full of water, and jump out of the city into the "country"!

The crime of 1407

IMPASSE DES ARBALÉTRIERS
38 RUE DES FRANCS-BOURGEOIS
Métro: Saint-Paul

Uneven paving stones, boundary stones, corbels – all, or almost all, characteristic of medieval streets – are to be found in the picturesque Impasse des Arbalétriers. It used to be the side entrance to the Barbette residence where Queen Isabeau of Bavaria (wife of Charles VI, King of France) lived in the early 14th century, and which no longer exists today. The path, now a cul-de-sac, led to a field where the crossbowmen used to train. Historians have it that Louis d'Orléans (brother of Charles VI and long-standing rival of Jean sans Peur) was assassinated by Jean's henchmen on this very spot on November 23rd, 1407, as he was returning from a visit to Queen Isabeau of Bavaria (see p. 16).

The cul-de-sac is not a true cul-de-sac as it leads to a vast courtyard which joins Rue Vieille-du-Temple.

A resting place for old stones

SQUARE GEORGES-CAIN
RUES PAYENNE, DU PARC-ROYAL AND DE SÉVIGNÉ
Métro: Saint-Paul

Until 1913, Hôtel Le Pelletier de Saint-Fargeau gardens used to be the site of a mail delivery station which delivered mail throughout most of Paris. The dark building deserved to be demolished, but the two doors with their curvilinear pediments most certainly did not. They opened directly onto the street, and served as a side entrance to the gardens in the 18th century.

The Square, a quiet spot today, is named after a former curator of the nearby Carnavalet Museum, which uses the place as a home for cumbersome old stones. You will find a clock pediment, fixed to the right-hand wall. It comes from the Tuileries Palace, burnt down in 1871. Just below the pediment is a carving of a group, dating back to the reign of Louis XIV (known as the Sun King), from the door of Château de Saint-Germain-en-Laye. You can also admire a ceiling rose taken from the former Paris City Hall, columns

from the Tuileries, and, in the middle of garden, a finely sculpted bronze statue which used to grace the Saint-Cloud gardens.

On the left, the ground-floor building bordering the Square was originally the Hôtel Le Pelletier de Saint-Fargeau orangery. Its central pediment is decorated with a representation of Truth, whose mirror, long gone, was angled towards the figure of an old man – a symbol of the destructive nature of Time – on the rear façade of the manor house at the far end of the Square.

The oldest house in Paris?

NICOLAS FLAMEL'S HOUSE
51 RUE DE MONTMORENCY
Métro: Rambuteau

historian, who researched the subject, to put an end to the legend in 1979. The house in Rue Volta proved to be nothing but a pastiche, built by a citizen of Paris in 1644.

Alas, the oldest house in Paris "only" dates from 1407! Its sombre, austere façade can be seen at 51 Rue de Montmorency, not very far from Rue Volta. The house was built by a certain Nicolas Flamel, a scribe at the University of Paris, who financed free lodgings for agricultural workers and fruit and vegetable growers from the neighbouring areas with rent collected from the shops on the ground floor.

The words engraved on the string course along the front wall, while the benefactor was still alive, continue to bear witness to that undertaking: "We men and women, living under the roof of this house built in the year fourteen hundred and seven, are in honour bound to recite one Paternoster and one Hail Mary every day, and to ask God, in His grace, to forgive the sins of the poor departed. Amen."

Flamel's initials can be seen on the pillars whose bas-relief sculptures, although restored in 1929, are in a very bad state today. *Ora et labora* ("pray and work") was the motto of Nicolas Flamel's house, the oldest in the capital... for the moment.

For a long time, the very medieval-looking house at 3 Rue Volta was thought to be the oldest house in Paris. All the books on the history of the city contained a picture with the following caption: "The oldest house in Paris", and postcards with the same title were printed in their thousands. It took the perseverance of a

A whispering gallery

CONSERVATORY OF ARTS AND CRAFTS
270-92 RUE SAINT-MARTIN
Opening hours: Monday to Friday, 1 to 8 pm, Saturday, 9 am to 7 pm. Métro: Arts-et-Métiers

The Conservatory of Arts and Crafts is not renowned for being the home of one the oldest monuments of Paris. Admittedly, the 19th-century style of the buildings in Rue Saint-Martin is deceiving; nevertheless, parts of one of the biggest and earliest abbeys of Paris can be seen here. Around 700, a basilica was built along an ancient road, later to become Rue Saint-Martin. After the Normans pillaged one of the monasteries in the 9th century, the place appears to have been abandoned until the middle of the 11th century when another abbey was founded, and rapidly developed into a large Benedictine monastery. Still standing on the corner of Rues du Vertbois and Saint-Martin is an imposing tower, a relic of the 13th-century wall. In the 19th century, because of a threat to demolish it, Victor Hugo was prompted into saying: "Demolish the tower? No! Demolish the architect? Yes!" Two fragments of the abbey wall, parts of a crenellated curtain wall, and a turret can be seen in Rue du Vertbois. Another tower serves as a well for a staircase at 7 Rue Bailly.

Beyond the entrance, on the right, stands a library with a glazed tile roof; it used to be the monastery refectory, built around 1230. Its rib vaults, supported by tall slender columns, are a marvel of ethereal grace.

Finally, a curious note to end your visit on. In the large hall where Lavoisier's laboratory equipment is on view, you might find it fun to stand at one corner of the hall, facing the wall, and whisper very softly to your "partner in crime" at the opposite corner of the room, also facing the wall. Unlike someone standing in the middle of the room, he will hear you very clearly. Legend has it that this was how the monks heard the confessions of people suffering from contagious diseases.

Crime on stage

THÉÂTRE LIBERTAIRE DE PARIS DÉJAZET
41 BOULEVARD DU TEMPLE
Métro: République

Cinema enthusiasts will be surprised to learn that a theatre, dating from the good old days of the "Boulevard of Crime", like the one portrayed in French film director Marcel Carné's film, *Les Enfants du Paradis* (Children of Paradise), has reopened its doors. Théâtre Libertaire de Paris Déjazet is the only theatre to have escaped Haussmann's city planning operations in 1862, when more than twenty were razed, wiping out one of the most fun-loving areas of Paris. Try to imagine, near the beginning of Boulevard du Temple, on the site of Place de la République, a road lined with theatres where tightrope walkers and mimes, first- and second-rate actors took part, nonstop, in light comedy and high tragedy. Crimes were "committed" on stage all along the boulevard to make the audiences cry.

Déjazet theatre used to be a royal tennis court, built by architect Belanger for Count d'Artois in 1786; the Louis Seize building overlooking the street is still there today, but without its pediment. It became, in turn, a bathhouse, a ballroom, and, finally, in 1842, a theatre, "Les Folies Meyer". Actress Virginie Déjazet, who excelled in male and female roles, bought the theatre in 1859, and had it named after her. Then, French playwright Victorien Sardou looked after it for a time.

After World War II, it became a cinema, and in 1986, when it was about to be closed down, Hervé Trinquier took out a lease in his name, and added the initials TLP – Théâtre Libertaire de Paris (Libertarian Theatre of Paris) – in memory of its former owner. Since then, one-man shows and musical comedies, in the grand tradition of Boulevard du Temple shows, are still put on. In an effort to revive the spirit of the past, the walls inside the theatre have been hung with funny frescoes – after Daumier, renowned, 19th-century painter and caricaturist – recalling the times when crime walked the streets of paradise.

The International in the Temple

14 RUE DE LA CORDERIE
Métro: Temple

A bend in Rue de la Corderie forms a picturesque square, lined with old buildings. It was formerly Cour de la Corderie, taken over by craftsmen in the 18th century, in the Temple enclosure.

Writer Jules Vallès declaimed: "Do you know the damp square between the Temple and Château-d'Eau (Place de la République), not far from the City Hall, boxed in by four rows of houses? Small shopkeepers occupy the ground floor, and their children play in the street. Carriages never come down here. The attics are full of poor people. This empty triangle is called Place de la Corderie. Take a good look at the house backing onto the faubourg barracks and overlooking the market. It looks quiet compared to the other houses. Go to the third floor and through a door, likely to fall off at the slightest knock of a shoulder, and enter a large, bare room, resembling a schoolroom. Greet the new Parliament! This is the revolution, sitting on the benches, leaning against the walls, resting its elbows on the rostrum, dressed in working men's clothes! This is where the International Working Men's Association holds its meetings, and the Fédération des Corporations Ouvrières (Federation of Working Men's Corporations) arranges to meet people."

Created in London in 1864, the International Working Men's Association was represented in Paris in 1865 at 44 Rue des Gravilliers. They moved several times because of frequent police searches before finally settling in at 14 Rue de la Corderie in 1869. The signal to start the Paris Commune (a Republican uprising against the Versailles government) was given here on February 16th, 1871.

Cité Dupetit-Thouars, an attractive cul-de-sac, is where Italian film director Luigi Comencini shot some of his film *La Bohème.*

Cité Dupetit-Thouars.

25

The Bastille in bits and pieces

PLACE DE LA BASTILLE, SQUARE HENRI-GALLI, BASSIN DE L'ARSENAL
Métro: Bastille and Sully-Morland

What's left of the Bastille fortress today? Very little indeed! No time was lost in razing it to the ground, and most of its stone was sold in order to build blocks of flats and the Pont de la Concorde.

Signs of the Bastille are negligible. Small, square paving stones at the start of Rue Saint-Antoine mark out

Square Henri-Galli.

its actual site, and at 3 Place de la Bastille, there is a map showing the exact position of the fortress, surrounded by formidable fortifications.

In 1898, an important discovery was made when the first métro

station was being built. The foundations of the tower of "liberty" were discovered between 211 and 236 Rue Saint-Antoine. They were dismantled, stone by stone, reassembled in Square Henri-Galli, and are still there today.

Another relic, part of the old moat wall now serving as a retaining wall for Boulevard Bourdon, can be seen at the junction of Canal Saint-Martin and Bassin de l'Arsenal, on the right-hand side looking towards the Seine. Inside the Bastille métro station, on the platform of line 5 going to Bobigny, some stones from the counterscarp wall of the Bastille moat are on view.

Finally, there are the "Bastille bells", installed in 1764. Later, they were saved from being melted down, and, for a short time, could be heard ringing in a café on the Place. Today, they belong to the State, and are on display in the Isle-Jourdain bell museum in the southwest department of Gers... a long way from the Bastille!

The wall of Philip Augustus

RUE DES JARDINS-SAINT-PAUL
Métro: Saint-Paul

Old buildings of the antique-dealer, "Saint-Paul village" area line one side of Rue des Jardins-Saint-Paul, while on the other, there is a piece of ground for sports activities, protected by a high wall complete with two towers. This is the largest relic of the enclosure built by Philip Augustus in 1190, more than eight centuries ago.

The wall owes its strength to the mixture of sand and rubble stone holding the outside facing stones together. The reason why so many parts of the enclosure were preserved throughout Paris is that rapid urban growth led to the absorption rather than the destruction of the fortifications, often used as supporting walls. Thus, several parts

of the wall can be seen – concealed and preserved – at the back of courtyards or workshops.

The 70-metre wall along Rue des Jardins-Saint-Paul is an impressive sight. To get an exact idea of how it looked in the Middle Ages, you have to imagine a wall with crenellations, somewhat higher than it is today.

The land is a matter of controversy between residents and city councillors. The City of Paris wants to build an underground car park and create a green area, which does not appeal to the residents. They would prefer to have sports facilities and a children's play area. Warfare, albeit on a small scale, in the shadows of Philip Augustus' towers...

Rendezvous under the elm

SAINT-GERVAIS ELM TREE
PLACE SAINT-GERVAIS
Métro: Hôtel-de-Ville

Have you ever noticed the elm tree in front of Saint-Gervais-Saint-Protais Church? Its history goes a long way back. Try to imagine the district as it was before Baron Haussmann's city planning began – a maze of old streets. They had quaint names such as Rues de la Tissanderie (weaving trade), de la Mortellerie (stone-breaking), du Pourtour (periphery), du Monceau (Monceaux village) – often referring to a craft, a physical characteristic, a locality – and were centred around Place Baudoyer, five times narrower than it is today. Rue Monceau opened out in front of the church to form a small square, in the middle of which the Saint-Gervais elm was planted, a little to the left of the present site. In the Middle Ages, people settled their differences under this tree, where they used to gather after Mass. Debts were paid and duels were arranged beneath its foliage. It was a convenient place to meet, and the expression: "Rendezvous under the elm" was familiar to Parisians for a long time. The Saint-Gervais factory used to finance the annual upkeep of the tree. History does not tell us what happened to the old elm tree, and it was not until March 10, 1914 that another one was planted.

The elm was often the subject of paintings and engravings, the most original of which can still be seen on the second-floor balconies of buildings adjoining the church (2-14 Rue François-Miron/17 Rue des Barres). Inside the houses, many firebacks are still ornamented with elms, which can also be found carved on four of the wooden choir stalls in Saint-Gervais Church.

An edge-tool maker's sign in Rue du Monceau was an elm, and, in the Carnavalet Museum, it continues to honour the memory of one of the most fragile monuments of Paris.

Some cannonball!

HÔTEL DE SENS (FORNEY LIBRARY)
1 RUE DU FIGUIER
Métro: Pont-Marie or Saint-Paul

The obvious penury of architecture around Hôtel de Sens, with its irregular silhouette, makes it seem quite out of place. Houses on the south side of Rue de l'Hôtel-de-Ville did not escape city planning of the fifties; some of them dated back to the 15th and 16th centuries, but were, nevertheless, demolished. Hôtel de Sens, built for the archbishops of Sens, is undoubtedly a survivor of the storm. Built in the 14th century, it was completely altered by Archbishop Tristan de Salazar in 1474.

In the late 17th century, it housed various artisans and commercial establishments. In the 18th century, stagecoaches to Dijon, Auxerre, Bar-sur-Aube, Belfort, and so on, used to leave from here. Then it became a laundry, a fruit and vegetable preserving factory, a rabbitskin cutting workshop, an optician's, a jam factory, and, finally, a glass factory.

When the City of Paris acquired it in 1911, it was very dilapidated; some of it had to be completely rebuilt in medieval style. The building was so thoroughly cleaned recently, that traces of a fresco (from a chapel which no longer exists) were washed off the walls overlooking the courtyard! One hot day in the revolutionary times of 1830, a stray, ill-fated cannonball embedded itself in the eastern façade of Hôtel de Sens. It is still there today, with the date of the event engraved underneath.

A multi-purpurse tower

SAINT-JACQUES TOWER
SQUARE DE LA TOUR SAINT-JACQUES
Métro: Châtelet

Tour Saint-Jacques (Saint James) is a well-known landmark, easy to recognize. This was also the case for pilgrims of Saint James who set off from here for Santiago de Compostela in Spain (world-famous pilgrimage in the Middle Ages, shrine of Saint James).

It used to be the bell-tower of Saint-Jacques-la-Boucherie Church, which took 25 years to build (1508-22). A large statue of Saint James was placed at the top to guide the pilgrims.

The French Revolution caused considerable damage to the church building. The tower's framework was burnt down in order to remove the bells, which, as they fell, smashed the vaults into pieces. The church was then sold to a man who demolished it, sparing only the tower.

A second-hand clothes market was set up on the site of the church, and the top of the tower was rented to a metal founder, who cleverly took advantage of its location by melting down the lead and pouring it from the top of the tower into a tub of water at the foot of building.

Repurchased in 1836 by the City of Paris, the tower was restored in 1852 by Ballu, who put the statues back on the top and the saints in their niches. A few years later, at the time of Haussmann's city-planning operations, the base of the tower was placed on a mound, underpinned, and had steps built around it. At that time, Pascal's statue, a reminder of the essays he wrote in 1648 on the weight of air, was installed under the archway. However, it was not under the Tour Saint-Jacques that the scientist and philosopher carried out his experiments, but in Saint-Jacques-du-Haut-Pas Church (5th arrondissement), but why quibble over a minor detail?

A meteorological station shares the top of the edifice with a few of kestrels who have taken up residence there!

Hidden treasure

RUE DU TRÉSOR
26 RUE VIEILLE-DU-TEMPLE
Métro: Saint-Paul

In 1882, while Hôtel d'Effiat was being demolished, a copper vase was unearthed from the rubble. It contained gold coins dating back to the reign of John II (King of France, 1350-64, known as John the Good) and to the reign of Charles V (King of France, 1364-80, known as Charles the Wise), the equivalent of 7,882 pounds of silver. When this treasure-trove was put up for sale, the Carnavalet Museum bought the vase and a few of the coins.

The road being built at the time, on the site of this manor house, was intended to create the junction between Rue Vieille-du-Temple and Rue des Écouffes; it was very aptly called "Rue du Trésor". Today, unidentified buildings line the cul-de-sac, with a 19th-century fountain abutting a relic of Hôtel Effiat at the far end. A door in the wall at the side opens into a passageway to Rue des Écouffes, and, around 1930, journalist Marius Richard described it as follows: "Let's continue our way through the passage whose doors are closed, or not, in the evening. The walls are all scraped and pitted by one wonders what... Those who live in the district must have very sharp elbows. Winter is the time to come down this narrow corridor, when a nasty wind blows in the rain, mingling with the light from the grimy gaslamp. However, the draughts may ambush and kill you."

Forever united

SITE OF THE HOUSE OF HÉLOÏSE AND ABELARD
9 QUAI AUX FLEURS
Métro: Hôtel-de-Ville

Who has not heard Héloïse and Abelard's distressing story of thwarted love? It has been told on stage so many times that the actors themselves have also become mythic figures. And yet this Parisian version of Romeo and Juliet really took place. Héloïse and Abelard met on Ile de la Cité.

A plaque on the approximate site of the lovers' residence on Quai aux Fleurs announces: "Ancienne habitation d'Héloïse et d'Abélard, 1118, rebâtie en 1849" (Former residence of Héloïse and Abelard, 1118, rebuilt in 1849). A little further on, you will see two 19th-century medallions bearing portraits of the immortal lovers.

Abelard, born in Nantes, arrived in Paris in 1100 to receive tuition from Guillaume de Champeaux. He became an eminent tutor, and readily accepted a request from Fulbert, canon at Notre-Dame, to give lessons to his niece, Héloïse. The young lady was 18 years old whereas Abelard was 39, but this did not stop pupil and tutor from falling passionately in love.

Fearing the canon's anger, the lovers fled to Brittany where they had a son before returning to Paris. Meanwhile, Fulbert had been preparing his revenge: he hired men to catch and castrate Abelard. From that time on, Abelard devoted himself entirely to spiritual matters; he became a monk and founded the Paraclete oratory. Héloïse became a nun at Argenteuil Convent.

On Abelard's death in the Saint-Marcel monastery of Châlon-sur-Saône in April 1142, Héloïse had his remains secretly transferred to the Paraclete. Twenty-two years later, Héloïse died and was buried beside Abelard in his coffin. The scandal was not discovered until centuries later when, in 1630, an abbess took it into her head to carefully sort and separate the lovers' bones.

Today, they are together again in Père Lachaise cemetery. Roses are regularly laid between the recumbent statues of Héloïse and Abelard, a sign of admiration for two lovers who were forced to part, and are now reunited forever.

The Golden Eagle Inn

CAFÉ DE LA GARE
41 RUE DU TEMPLE
Métro: Rambuteau

Poet and precursor of surrealism, Guillaume Apollinaire was an unrepentant "stroller on both banks", and particularly liked the austere, evocative atmosphere of the Golden Eagle Inn in Rue du Temple. Today, the building houses Café de la Gare Theatre and dance studios. In the 19th century, it was a coach inn, and the courtyard used to have an enormous shelter for the coaches and carriages that stopped there.

Entering the courtyard, you will see a magnificent Louis Treize staircase on your right. The courtyard looks surprisingly majestic beneath its grimy exterior. In fact, in the 17th century, the old inn was a beautiful manor house, and what remains today are the main body of building and its left wing. Despite the lack of upkeep, there are still a few interesting relics. In 1971, some splendid Louis Treize ceilings with painted beams were discovered on the first floor of the main building, and are visible from the courtyard.

The dilapidated state of the place calls to mind the postwar Marais district, where fine residences, occupied by a working population, used to house garages, workshops and various craft industries, a factor which helped save them from demolition, and, since the sixties, often brought about their restoration.

A medieval house – true or false?

1 RUE DES CHANTRES/1-3 RUE DES URSINS
Métro: Hôtel-de-Ville or Cité

A house on the corner of Rue des Chantres and Rue des Ursins attracts attention because it looks very old. It is one of the rare houses to escape Baron Haussmann's city-planning operations which destroyed much of Ile de la Cité, except for Place Dauphine and a few streets near Notre-Dame.

This house down by the quay was still a funny, oddly-shaped little place when architect Fernand Pouillon began to restore it in 1958. In fact, the architect transformed it into a curious copy of a medieval house, as he recounts in his memoirs: "After a year's work, the ruin, demolished bit by bit, was replaced by a clever pastiche of deliberately ill-assorted architectural items, which have been both envied and admired ever since by people dreaming of a view over the Seine."

The originality of the house lies in the splendid antique pieces, of various origins, which Fernand Pouillon incorporated into his building. Some of them can be seen from the street (stained-glass windows, wrought-iron bars). Also to be noted are the tower-cum-stairwell, the two mullioned windows to the right of the steps, and the door at the top of the steps in Rue des Ursins, all very medieval-looking.

The architect lived for only a year in this amazing house, which was then occupied by the Aga Khan. Today, the small house in Rue des Chantres blends in with the scenery; although not an ancient dwelling, it is a real masterpiece by a talented architect.

Tombstones to keep your feet dry

26, RUE CHANOINESSE
Métro: Cité

At the heart of one of the rare spots spared by Baron Haussmann, Rue Chanoinesse is reminiscent of the cloister of Notre-Dame, where the canons, safe inside a closed, guarded domain until the 18th century, were able to dedicate their lives to work and meditation. Canons used to live at nos. 22 and 24, buildings which open into the street via two wide doorways leading to courtyards. The latter building now bears the façade of an authentic, 18th-century, wine merchant's shop, and you can still taste the juice of the vine here, as a restaurant, "Vieux Paris", keeps up the tradition.

At no. 26, there is a small, narrow courtyard common to several buildings. In the past, this may have been a passageway into Rue des Ursins, and has become a cul-de-sac today. It is lined with reused columns. However, the main interest of the place lies in the long flagstones on the ground, on which traces of Gothic script can be detected. These flagstones are, in fact, tombstones from some religious establishment on Ile de la Cité. They were used for drainage, and as a result, generations of Parisians, without much regard for the deceased, were able to keep their feet dry!

A 17th-century métro station

THE VAULTS OF CHÂTELET MÉTRO STATION
(LINE 7 TO LA COURNEUVE, EXIT RUE SAINT-MARTIN)

Vaults slightly higher than the tunnel can be seen from the platform at Châtelet métro station. The fact that they date back to the 17th century makes them the oldest work of art of the entire Paris métro!

In 1642, on this very spot, Louis XIII parted with a piece of land between Pont Notre-Dame and Pont au Change. The only obligation incumbent upon the new owner, the Marquess of Gesvres, was to build a quay supported by a series of arches. Well situated, overlooking the Seine, the quay rapidly became a haunt for pickpockets and other disreputable individuals. In 1860, its openings were walled in, and its sunny, sheltered spots, afforded by the vaults built in front of the port, were

forgotten. Only a few engravings and a painting by Hubert Robert (18th-century painter and engraver) serve as a reminder of the existence of those dark galleries.

Around 1921, engineers discovered the old vaults on the edge of the Seine while working on the site of the Ivry-Villette métro line. The rubble, piping, and sewer outlets obstructing them were carefully cleared out, and, at the request of the experts on the City Committee for Old Paris, the vaults were preserved. They are still there today, and the best view of them is from the footbridge between the two platforms. Reproductions of 18th-century engravings of those sunny, sheltered spots are also on show.

Imperial bees

NOTRE-DAME-DE-PARIS MUSEUM
10 RUE DU CLOÎTRE-NOTRE-DAME
Open on Wednesdays, Saturdays and certain public holidays. Tel: 01.43.25.42.92. Métro: Cité

Notre-Dame-de-Paris is one of the most visited monuments in the capital, and yet most people are unaware that it has a museum. Tucked away in the archbishop's palace are three tiny rooms where the exhibits recall the glorious past of the cathedral. One of the first Merovingian cathedrals used to occupy the present site. Some of its remains were discovered in 1847 and 1965. Past history is vividly recalled by items such as the base of a small glass dish with a "chrismon" showing through, the earliest evidence of the conversion of Paris to Christianity.

Until the 19th century, a small, narrow street used to lead up to the front of the cathedral, and its cellars were explored by archeologists. A faience pot found there, bearing the inscription, "buvé a la providence" (drink to providence), must have been used at the nearby Hôtel-Dieu during the 17th century.

Original drawings, engravings and paintings give an account of the cathedral's setting throughout the ages, going back to the time when episcopal buildings occupied the end of the island; the church district was closed in the evening and had its own police force. There are paintings, the oldest dating back to the 17th century, depicting the interior of the edifice before the French Revolution: no chairs in the nave and lots of statues, paintings and tapestries, of which only a few dispersed relics remain today. All that is left of the decoration created for the crowning of Napoleon I (Napoleon Bonaparte) are two gilded bronze bees.

These clearly-presented, both humble and valuable pieces help us to understand the extent to which the cathedral was an essential part of Paris and the real "heart" of the capital.

Below are the chrismon and the last of the Emperor's coronation bees.

They sell horses, don't they?

THE FORMER HORSE MARKET
5 AND 11-13 RUE GEOFFROY-SAINT-HILAIRE
Métro: Saint-Marcel

A century ago, there were about 80,000 horses in the capital, putting Paris ahead of the Meuse, the most "horsy" department in the country. The Boulogne draught-horses walked along the quays pulling heavy loads, the Percherons trotted by with omnibuses in tow, the Anglo-Normans' proudly pounded along the streets of the uptown districts.

The big Paris horse market, decided upon by Louis XIII in 1641, used to stand on the present site of Boulevard Saint-Marcel and Boulevard de l'Hôpital, where it remained until 1908, when it was transferred to the Vaugirard slaughterhouses.

The market was supervised from a building at 5 Rue Geoffroy-Saint-Hilaire, which can be seen from Boulevard Saint-Marcel. This lovely Louis Quinze house was built between 1760 and 1762, under the orders of Police Lieutenant General Sartine. On either side of the centre window, a crane and a cock, symbols of patience and vigilance, stand face to face.

At nos. 11 to 13, the inscription on the façade beneath the head of a horse declares the following: "Dealers in thoroughbreds, ponies of all kinds and shire horses." This building, along with the house at no. 5, is all that remains of the market.

The hospital bakery

HÔTEL SCIPION
13 RUE SCIPION
Métro: Gobelins

Square Scipion with its low-roofed houses has been miraculously preserved. It was widened and restructured in 1985, and is ornamented with a large, terracotta, low-relief sculpture by Alexandre Charpentier, a reminder of the bakery trade.

Opposite stands the solidly-built façade of a 17th-century building with tall windows and wrought-iron work. The centre door has a round opening with a grille over it, bearing the following inscription "s(ainte) Marthe, maison de Scipion" (Saint Marthe, House of Scipion). If you push open the door, you will find yourself in a big courtyard, similar to that of a coach house because of its width. The right wing, more low-roofed and older than the rest, is an outstanding, very well restored Renaissance edifice. It has stone arches on the ground floor, and, on the floor above, terracotta medallions, casts of the original medallions kept in the Public Health and Welfare Museum, which, until a few years ago, was housed here.

The Central Bakery for Paris hospitals used to occupy these buildings (since the 17th century), which explains why there is so much space and why the entrance is so exceptionally high.

The manor house was built in the 16th century for a certain Maurice de Bullioud, and then bought by Scipion Sardini, hence the name. The Genoese gentleman's sympathies were with Catherine de Médicis and Henry II, and he was probably responsible for having the terracotta medallions installed on the façade of the right wing. No serious claims as to the making of these medallions have been recorded. Some mention the Juste atelier (family of 16th-century sculptors renowned for their ornamental, Renaissance style), but do not provide much in the way of proof to support their theories.

In 1613, the manor house was rented to a mental hospital for the poor, then it served as a baby-farm for the children of needy families, before becoming an apprentices' workshop and tapestry factory.

Rue des Marionnettes

277 AND 284 RUE SAINT-JACQUES
RER: Port-Royal

A t no. 284 Rue Saint-Jacques, opposite the magnificent Val-de-Grâce, an unusual relic of old Paris is hidden away in a modern building behind a pane of glass: a stone portal which, until the French Revolution, served as an entrance to the convent of the Incarnation Carmelites. When the apartment block was built in 1978, the portal as well as a small manor house, which can be seen from 6 Rue du Val-de-Grâce, were in danger of disappearing. As a result of various protests, the *tabula rasa* enthusiasts were urged to exercise restraint; the portal was dismantled, stone by stone, and reassembled in the place where you can see it today. The manor house, built for sculptor François

Scelles in 1796, was also saved. It has an attractive façade, crowned with balusters. During excavation works, vaulted, underground channels were discovered near the cellars of the manor house. They were part of the system which carried water from Arcueil to a fountain in Rue Saint-Jacques, known as the "Carmelites' Fountain".

At no. 277, through one of the two houses flanking Val-de-Grâce Chapel, there is a paved alley, lined with guardstones and ending in a cul-de-sac. This used to be Rue des Marionnettes, formerly linking Rue de l'Arbalète with Rue Saint-Jacques. The passage of time does not appear to have affected this old street, a veritable fossil of a road.

The living and the dead

SAINT-SÉVERIN CHARNEL HOUSE
RUE DES PRÊTRES-SAINT-SÉVERIN
Métro: Cluny-La Sorbonne/RER: Saint-Michel

The rare visitors to a little square next to Saint-Séverin Church may notice some singular-looking Gothic buildings at the far end on the right. This curved corridor with its pointed roofs is not a cloister but a charnel house used in former times to deposit remains from the communal grave that used to exist on this site. It is the only one left in the entire city.

The charnel house was built in the late 15th century around the Saint-Séverin cemetery. It was customary for the dignitaries of the parish to be interred beneath the arcades, while the draughty space under the roofs was reserved for "less high-ranking" corpses taken from the communal grave.

However, at Saint-Séverin, the living very soon took over from the dead. In the 17th century, some of the arcades were filled in with stained glass so that the churchwardens could hold their meetings there, and lodgings were installed for the priests above one of the arcades.

By the 18th century, the disused cemetery was surrounded by nothing but blind arcades, blocked up by stone walls. In 1840, some of them were demolished to make way for a presbytery. It was not until 1920 that the remaining vaults were restored by architect Bévière.

The last rood-screen

SAINT-ÉTIENNE-DU-MONT CHURCH
1 PLACE SAINTE-GENEVIÈVE
RER: Luxembourg

A rood-screen, the only one of its kind in Paris, lies hidden within the walls of Saint-Étienne-du-Mont Church. It was used for reading from the Gospel, before the pulpit was created. When pulpits had completely supplanted rood-screens, the latter were usually destroyed.

In the middle of the 18th century, some parishioners from Montagne Sainte-Geneviève demanded that the Saint-Étienne-du-Mont rood-screen be demolished. One of them even offered three thousand silver pounds to pay for the job! Despite the lightness of the structure concealing the chancel, members of the congregation most enamoured of modernism felt the structure was improper. Fortunately, Providence intervened; ardent reformers were discouraged from destroying a rood-screen which is still in almost perfect condition.

Antoine Beaucorps built this marvel in 1541. Essentially Renaissance, the rood-screen comprises one 9-metre, depressed, basket-handle arch on the transept side, and three archways joined by two slender pillars on the chancel side, and is designed so as to leave the nave in full view. You will appreciate the sculpture on the two flights of steps on either side of the platform with its ornamental openwork balustrade. In the corner-pieces of the arch facing the transept, the two winged female figures used to carry the nails of the Passion and the Crown of Thorns, symbols which were replaced by a crown of olive and oak leaves in 1794. Notice also the beautiful pulpit, as well as the organ case, dating back to 1630.

From Bernardine monks to policemen

THE FORMER BERNARDINE COLLEGE
18-24 RUE DE POISSY
Métro: Maubert-Mutualité

One of the most noteworthy relics of medieval Paris, the refectory of the Bernardine college, is still standing in Rue de Poissy. The College was founded in 1244 by the Englishman, Étienne de Lexington, Abbot of Clairvaux. The institution was taken over by Cîteaux Abbey in 1320, and reconstruction work was carried out in 1336. All that remains today is the "papal abode" which survived demolition when Rues de Poissy and de Pontoise (1806) and Boulevard Saint-Germain (1855) were built.

The layout of the "papal abode" may be admired from Rue de Poissy. Its basement is supported by ogival vaults, the ground floor has arches, and the upper floor used to serve as the students' dormitory. The gothic arched windows of the former refectory (with adjoining classrooms), the small chapterhouse, and the kitchen are framed by large buttresses.

The basement, regularly flooded by the Seine, was filled in by the Bernardines in 1709. About twenty years ago, when it was cleared out, 32 sturdy pillars on octagonal bases were discovered, placed at regular intervals in this 80 x 15 metre room.

In 1698, the first floor was destroyed by fire, and clumsily rebuilt. The roof of the former edifice was higher and more sharp-angled. Only one of the two gables remains, and is ornamented with a rose on the north side. The place was used for various purposes, which did nothing to improve its condition. In turn, it became a street lamp oil shop, an archive room for the City of Paris, and premises for the Frères des Écoles Chrétiennes (the Brothers of Christian Schools). Between 1845 and 1993, it was used as a fire station.

The former sacristy at 18 Rue de Poissy, which linked the refectory and the church, dates back to the 14th century. A beautiful door can be seen in the courtyard at 27 Boulevard Saint-Germain.

As was requested by the City Committee for Old Paris, the firemen vacated the buildings. However, the unusual combination of new tenants – an association for the music of Notre-de-Dame-de-Paris and a dormitory for police auxiliaries – is hardly any more in keeping with the site.

The Thirty-Three at no. 34!

THE FORMER SEMINARY OF THE THIRTY-THREE
RUE DE LA MONTAGNE-SAINTE-GENEVIÈVE
Métro: Cardinal-Lemoine

scholarship holders, the number referring to the age of Christ when he died.

The part overlooking the street was built by Germain-Éloi Legrand in 1737. At the far end of the courtyard, architect Charon erected an elegant building with big arcades. The upper stories are reached by a staircase, with a wrought-iron balustrade, down which we can imagine the seminarists racing after classes. A curious feature is the tiny door, between the ground and the first floor, leading to the other side of the college and giving access to Impasse des Bœufs.

A heavy, 18th-century door opens into a passage leading to a courtyard resembling a small street. Unevenly paved alleys lead up to buildings of different heights.

This is the Seminary of the Thirty-Three, established in 1657 in the former Hôtel d'Albiac. This little-known college of the Latin Quarter gets its name from its thirty-three

The smaller buildings, although added during the 19th century, blend in well with those around them.

As the evening darkness begins to fall, the courtyard of the Thirty-Three, under the pale lamplight, gives you an idea of Paris as it used to be in the 18th century with its twisting, mysterious alleys.

Down below, on the mountain...

ROCK GARDEN IN JARDIN DES PLANTES
RUE JUSSIEU/RUE GEOFFROY-SAINT-HILAIRE
The rock garden is open from April to September. Métro: Jussieu

The little rock garden does not immediately spring into view as you first glance over the vast Jardin des Plantes. The reason for such unobtrusiveness is because this delightful place is a sunken garden, located three metres below the terraced gardens in order to create hilly ground, a feature which is altogether untypical of the neat flower-beds of Jardin des Plantes.

At the beginning of the thirties, the Museum botanists came up with the idea of presenting mountain plants in the heart of the capital, in surroundings as similar as possible to those of their natural environment. The undertaking had its complications as the plants grown in the garden did not all originate from the same part of the world. The ambition was to cultivate both mountain flora as well as plants from the Mediterranean areas. Light, warmth, humidity, soil types – each plant requiring specific conditions which could not be left to chance.

The garden is protected from sudden changes in weather conditions and from harsh winds, thanks to its hollowed out terraces and the big trees along Allée Cuvier and in the nearby zoo. The gardeners make the most of the northern or southern exposures and the permanently shady areas of this little, sheltered valley. Over just a few metres, temperatures can range from 15 to 20°C, what one would call a microclimate! More than 2,000 plants from the Alps, the Pyrenees, Corsica, as well as the Himalayas, Japan and China, all cultivated on a few acres of rock garden with little streams running through it, appear to appreciate this sanctuary in the heart of Paris.

If you go through the underground passage which starts in the Botanic School gardens and crosses Allée Cuvier, you will come up into the heart of the rock garden, between the Cévennes massif and that of the Pre-Alps. Columbines, cornflowers, foxgloves, alpine sea holly and asters bring touches of bright colour to these massifs, whose most precious flower remains the edelweiss, the "star of the snows", an uncommon sight in Parisian parks and squares. Opposite, along the zoo wall, there are rocks from the Balkans and the Mediterranean, scattered with lavender and rosemary. On the same side, towards the far end of the garden, you will see the massifs of the Caucasus and Corsica as well as rocks from Japan and China, and as you return to the entrance you will go past rocks from the Himalayas, North America and the Pyrenees. Opposite the Pyrenees massif, in the middle of the garden, stand the rocks sheltering cacti and succulents.

Towards Rue Geoffroy-Saint-Hilaire, behind the greenhouses, you can still see the Coypeau hillock, originally a dumping ground in medieval times. The iron and bronze gazebo at the top was built in 1786 by the garden ironsmith, according to Verniquet's plans. This is one of the first iron structures in the world, all the more exceptional since this was more than half a century before the achievements of Victor Baltard, also a forerunner in that area (he built the main buildings for Les Halles market). Beneath the cornice, there is an inscription in latin: horas non numero nisi serenas *(I only count the hours of happiness). It refers to an ingenious device, no longer here today, that used to tell the time according to the sun. It consisted of a small Chinese drum placed in the hollow of a globe at the top of the belvedere. A horsehair thread, burnt under a magnifying glass set according to the meridian, triggered off a clock mechanism which struck the drum at midday. Naturally, the horsehair thread had to be changed every day!*

Circus games

LUTETIA ARENAS
49 RUE MONGE/RUE DES ARÈNES
Métro: Cardinal-Lemoine

erected along Rue Monge accounted for the disappearance of a good third of the arenas.

It was not until 1883, after a vigorous campaign led by Victor Hugo and Victor Duruy, that the last remains of the arenas were discovered. They were finally restored in 1917-18.

The last remains of the great Lutetia arenas, long since buried underground, are hidden away in the middle of a square. And yet, those arenas, nearly nineteen centuries old, have never really been forgotten; even people living in Middle Ages used to talk about the "enclosure of the arenas". Memories of them only began to fade when the ground on the site was levelled off, making their exact location increasingly uncertain. In 1869, the underlying remains of the arenas were discovered. However, despite the efforts of a very active Society for the Arenas, the site was filled in, and a depot installed for the Omnibus Company. Buildings

The amphitheatre and its stage were built on the slope of Montagne Sainte-Geneviève at the beginning of the 2nd century. This meant that many of the tiers could be built into the hillside itself. The steps surrounding an oval arena faced a big podium equipped with a wall with recesses where a succession of different kinds of entertainment could be presented: circus games, mime, drama, and so on. In its time, this amphitheatre was the second biggest circus in Gaul before its decline towards the 4th century, when it served as a quarry for the inhabitants of the area.

A chapel in bits and pieces

SQUARE LAURENT-PRACHE
RUE DE L'ABBAYE
Métro: Saint-Germain-des-Prés

Saint-Germain-de-Prés Church is the relic of an abbey of the same name, one of the most imposing abbeys in France. After two of its bell-towers had been knocked down during the French Revolution, and it had been converted into a saltpetre factory in the late 19th century, the church was in such a bad state that work to restore – and change the nature of – the edifice was undertaken several times during the 19th century. However, our main interest here concerns the relics outside in Square Laurent-Prache. Exposed to the wind and the rain, the remains of a magnificent chapel, dedicated to the Virgin Mary, have been on view here since the beginning of the century. Perpendicular to the site of Rue de l'Abbaye, this jewel of a chapel was built in 1255 by the famous architect, Pierre de Montreuil, who was buried here some years later alongside his wife. The French Revolution left the chapel practically unscathed, whereas it was dealt a fatal blow during the 19th century. After serving as a granary, the chapel was restored to the church for the purpose of worship from 1795 to 1802, the year when Dr Salbrune bought and razed it to the ground. He saved a few architectural items which he installed on the façade of his house, a strange way of paying tribute to a building he had just destroyed.

After his house was demolished at the beginning of this century, some of the chapel's relics were recovered and placed in the square bordering Saint-Germain-des-Prés Church, making it a veritable museum of stones. Since then, there has been a general lack of concern regarding this beautiful chapel's remains, which continue to deteriorate.

The door of the edifice can be seen in Cluny Museum gardens, and, fortunately, a stained-glass window has been preserved, its kaleidoscope of colours glowing in one of the apses of Saint-Germain-des-Prés Church.

Saint Vincent de Paul's shrine

CHAPEL OF THE PRIESTS OF THE LAZARIST MISSION
95 RUE DE SÈVRES
Mondays to Saturdays: 7-11.30 am/1.30-6.30 pm. Sundays: 8-12 am/1.30-3.15 pm. Métro: Vaneau

The stained-glass windows give a picture-book account of the life of Saint Vincent de Paul. Born on April 24th, 1581 in Pouy, near Dax, he was ordained priest in 1600, and devoted his life to both study and adventure. Captured during one of his journeys, he was sold as a slave in Tunis. He converted his master, escaped, and returned to Paris. He became chaplain to Queen Marguerite de Valois (whose marriage to the future Henry IV was one of the causes of the massacre of Saint Bartholomew's Day), then parish priest in Clichy-la-Garenne, before becoming private tutor to the illustrious Gondi family. In 1617, moved by the poverty he saw around him, he founded the "Brotherhood of Charity" in Châtillon-les-Dombes; people throughout the world benefited from it. "Mr Vincent" died on September 27th, 1660 and was canonized by Pope Clement XII on June 16th, 1737.

The Lazarists' chapel, with its rather plain, pedimented façade, is a fine, recently-restored, 19th-century building. As a replacement for the Saint-Lazare priory (Rue du Faubourg-Saint-Denis) after the French Revolution, the priests of the Mission were given the former Hôtel de Lorges. The chapel you see today was built on part of that site (1826-27).

The interesting items in this chapel include a Cavaillé-Coll organ, a series of paintings by "Brother François", pupil of Ingres, and, above all, a silver shrine, visible as soon as you enter, in which the relics of Saint Vincent de Paul are preserved.

A staircase concealed in the masonry affords a good view of this exceptional piece of silverwork, created by silversmith Odiot in 1830. The 2.25m by 0.65m shrine contains a wax statue, dressed in priestly garments and holding a cross which Vincent may have used to comfort Louis XIII during the last hours of his life.

Bloodshed at the Carmelite monastery

SAINT-JOSEPH-DES-CARMES
74 RUE DE VAUGIRARD
Métro: Saint-Placide

T he beautiful, domed façade of Saint-Joseph Church can be seen at the far end of a courtyard through a metal gate. On the right, a passageway gives easy access to the door into the building, hidden from view.

The Carmelites, originally from Spain, settled in Paris in the early 17th century. During the 18th century, the monastery in Rue de Vaugirard was extended between Rues du Regard, du Cherche-Midi and Cassette. The monks cultivated the herbs for the famous lemon balm water (marketed under the name of "Eau des Carmes Boyer") in their enormous garden. However, this peaceful, rural life was to be disrupted by bloodshed.

As a result of the law of

August 17th, 1792, whereby all the monasteries had to be vacated, the Carmelite monastery was converted into a prison. More than 150 priests refusing to take an oath to uphold the Constitution were imprisoned there.

As the Prussian army advanced, so revolutionary fervour mounted in Paris; the prisoners were accused of spying for the enemy, and their heads were demanded by the revolutionary Saint-Sulpice branch. On September 2nd, 1792, armed men led by citizen Maillard entered the prison screaming for the death of the prisoners. The massacre lasted three days. After a sham trial, pikes, swords and makeshift weapons were used to kill 118 monks in the gardens near the steps, still there today. In the crypt, there is a very dramatic presentation of the remains of these men, disinterred from a grave that had been dug in the garden. A macabre detail: not a single skull is in one piece. On the upper floor in one of the former cells, a relic – traces of blood from the executioners' pikes – is protected by a wooden frame.

Courtyard-cum-garden

ZADKINE MUSEUM
100 BIS RUE D'ASSAS
Open every day except Mondays and public holidays from 10 am to 5.40 pm. RER: Port-Royal

A narrow passageway between some tall buildings leads to the entrance of the secluded Zadkine museum at the far end of a courtyard-cum-garden.

Ossip Zadkine lived here from 1928 until his death in 1967. Born in Russia in 1890, he arrived in Paris at the age of nineteen. To begin with, he lived in La Ruche (see p. 139), then in Rue de Vaugirard and Rue Rousselet, and, in 1920, he exhibited his work for the first time. This success was followed by others; Zadkine exhibited forty-seven sculptures at the 1937 International Exhibition, and went to New York in the same year to show his work to the Brummer gallery.

Zadkine returned to New York to escape from the Nazis during the World War II, and devoted a lot of his time to teaching. His work, very much in the public eye, was the subject of a retrospective held in the National Modern Art Museum in 1949.

Apart from Zadkine's work, a walk in this garden in Rue d'Assas brings to mind the countless other little backyards where Montparnasse artists, the famous "Montparnos", lived and worked before World War II.

The sculptor's secluded, 19th-century home was converted into several small exhibition rooms. Contemplating Zadkine's sculptures – skilful entanglements of shapes in wood, stone or bronze – is a moving experience. The original, poignant plaster cast of the monument dedicated to Vincent van Gogh is a masterpiece of sensitivity.

There is a welcoming bench in the garden where statues of all sizes have been installed, often by Zadkine himself. Mingling with the trees and the ivy, his work – sober, sensual, and out of the ordinary – is a tribute to nature.

The revolutionary metre

36 RUE DE VAUGIRARD (TO THE RIGHT OF THE PORCH UNDER THE ARCHES)
RER: Luxembourg

Defined as the ten-millionth part of the meridian circle between the North Pole and the Equator, the metre was brought in by the Convention (responsible for the Proclamation of the Republic in 1792) in 1795 to replace the toise and the foot. The creation of a common unit was really revolutionary when you think that, under the *Ancient Régime*, the foot was divided into a variable number of inches, and represented different lengths depending on where you lived.

Adopting the metre meant mastering the decimal system, not an easy task in view of the degree of illiteracy in France at the time. People could divide by 2, 4 or 8, by folding a piece of string once, twice or three times, but dividing by 10 was quite different matter!

In order to acquaint the public with the new unit of measure, 16 marble standard metres were installed in the busiest parts of Paris between February 1796 and December 1797.

There are only two left in Paris today, and only one is in its original position in Rue de Vaugirard. It is fixed to the wall of a private manor house taken over by the Department of Weights and Measures at the end of the 18th century.

Nothing but a sharp chill...

COUR DE ROHAN
RUE DU JARDINET/COUR DU COMMERCE-SAINT-ANDRÉ
Métro: Odéon

The narrow Rue du Jardinet snakes between buildings up to the gates of Cour de Rohan, a peaceful, green space in an area devoted to tourism. The former, well-restored manor house, wrongly attributed to the archbishops of Rouen, has three small courtyards. The first one, Louis Treize in character, built in brick and stone, has a well in a recess on the left, complete with well-curb, gargoyle and pulley. A passage leads to the second courtyard where there is a wrought-iron mounting-block, the last one in Paris; ladies, abbots and old men used it to mount their horses.

In the third courtyard, a fragment of Philip Augustus' wall forms a

A quite spot away from the noisy boulevards.

terrace, which used to be the end of Rue du Jardinet, a cul-de-sac until 1791. Since the end of the 18th century, a wide door gives access to Cour du Commerce-Saint-André, just opposite the rear entrance of the famous "Procope" café. This passage was partly destroyed when Boulevard Saint-Germain was built; it used to join an old street, Rue des Cordeliers, near Danton's statue.

Danton and his wife lived in the house at the top of the passage which Danton used to take to go to the "Procope", long renowned for its passionate debating sessions.

Marat set up the *l'Ami du Peuple* printing works at no. 8, now a recently renovated shop, where, on the left at the back, you can see the base of one of the towers of Philip Augustus' wall (see p. 27).

At no. 9, sheep were used to test the guillotine, a revolutionary tool which, according to its inventor, Dr Guillotin, would "standardize" methods used for putting the condemned to death. The doctor, a humanist when the fancy took him, asserted that the heavy blade sliding rapidly down between the two wooden uprights would painlessly cut off the heads of the prisoners, "who would feel nothing but a sharp chill on the nape of the neck".

Revolution at the convent

REFECTORY OF THE FORMER CORDELIER CONVENT
15 RUE DE L'ÉCOLE-DE-MÉDECINE
Métro: Odéon

organized around a church, built in 1262 and the biggest in Paris since it covered the area occupied by today's School of Medicine. Building work on the refectory itself began in the second half of the 15th century, and was completed in 1506.

However, the Cordelier Convent (the monks got their name from the knotted cord girdles they wore) is known more for its extra-theological activities. In the spring of 1790, the famous Cordeliers' Club, one of the most important political clubs of the French Revolution, began holding their public meetings here. More left-wing than the Jacobins (radical political group led by Robespierre during the French Revolution), the Cordeliers were led by Danton and Marat who lived nearby. Marat, who lived at no. 20, was buried in the monastery garden after his fatal meeting with Charlotte Corday.

Behind a small metal door to the left of the main entrance, there are some 17th- and 18th-century graffitti on the walls between the 8th and 10th buttresses. They are highlighted by a very symbolic palm leaf, and immortalize the names of the monks connected with the school of convent theology.

The refectory, all that is left of the Cordelier Convent, is a fine example of flamboyant Gothic architecture, a rare sight in Paris. Founded by Franciscan monks in the 13th century, the convent was

Opposite: An outside view of the convent.
Above: The former refectory.

The house of retorts

25 BOULEVARD DU MONTPARNASSE
Métro: Montparnasse-Bienvenüe

The façade overlooking the garden.

In the 18th century, Rue de Vaugirard wound its way past huge properties, with beautiful French-style gardens, and more modest, country cottages. Montparnasse was still a hillock with muddy paths zigzagging up and down.

The residence at 25 Boulevard du Montparnasse is a fine example of that period. Now in disrepair and heightened by several storeys, it used to be surrounded, in the days of its glory, by a small park opening onto Rue de Vaugirard through a heavy portal.

On the south side, go through a double wrought-iron gate into a tiny courtyard where you can admire, unfortunately too close-up, the classic layout of the façade ornamented with delicate-looking *mascarons*. You can get a good view of the entire north side of the manor house from the courtyard at no. 23.

The house was built in 1712, and a certain Catherine Bonot became its owner the following year. After that, there was a succession of occupiers: Count de Béthune followed by Prince de Condé in 1716, and then Philippe de Vendôme in 1722. Philippe de Vendôme, a renowned libertine and brother of the Duke de Vendôme, was France's Grand Prior of the Knights of Malta. A high-ranking dignitary ruling supreme over the Temple and its members, later to be scorned by Louis XIV, Philippe ended his life in his manor house in Rue de Varenne, cheated and ruined by his servants, and deserted by all those who had loved him during his hours of glory.

What was he doing in Rue de Vaugirard, when his real home was in Rue de Varenne? Like many of his contemporaries, he was perhaps trying to discover the key to the philosopher's stone.

On Philippe de Vendôme' s death in 1727, the notaries, while making an inventory of the deceased's belongings, discovered a room full of retorts, flasks and filters, the tools of someone dabbling in the exalting, if not exact, sciences.

The time according to Saint-Sulpice

THE CHURCH GNOMON
PLACE SAINT-SULPICE
Métro: Saint-Sulpice

Outstanding in many ways, Saint-Sulpice Church has a gnomon – a somewhat worldly item for a church – in the left wing of its transept. The white marble, astronomical measuring instrument is an obelisk with a line of copper leading away from it, embedded in the floor. When the sun shines, the ingenious device indicates the "true" midday hour and the approximate date.

Completed in 1727, the meridian line was improved upon by Pierre Lemonnier in 1744. In order to use it in winter as well, he built an obelisk ten metres high, linking it with the gnomon's eye located 25 metres above the ground in a transept window facing south. The copper line embedded in the floor is meant to represent the Paris meridian, the accuracy of which people with a rational turn of mind are quick to contest. What does it matter, as long as the time spent wandering round the square is a happy time!

A museum of stones

ÉCOLE DES BEAUX-ARTS
14 RUE BONAPARTE
Métro: Saint-Germain-des-Prés

Convent, that archeologist Alexandre Lenoir stored works of art which he managed to rescue from the hands of the revolutionaries, thus creating the first Museum of French Monuments. Various pieces of architecture, statues, medieval tombs were on view to the public in the "Élysée Garden", the latter making a considerable impression on generations of young romantics, many of whom became artists or writers. The museum was closed in 1816, and became the School of Fine Arts.

Conversion work on the former convent was started by architect François Debret, and continued by Félix Duban until 1872. He installed pieces of architecture from the former museum all over the school, and some of them can still be seen in the main courtyard.

The architect placed the central projecting part of Anet Castle, built by Philibert Delorme for Diane de Poitiers, on the right-hand side of the church façade. The gates in front also came from the castle. Opposite, under the arches, are some of the remains of the magnificent Hôtel Legendre, built during the 15th and 16th centuries and demolished in 1844. Remains of the Tuileries are also scattered about.

The School of Fine Arts opens into Rue Bonaparte through a wide courtyard surrounded by austere, 19th-century buildings. The school's various, easily accessed courtyards are havens of peace in the heart of Paris.

It was here, in the gardens, among the relics of the Grands-Augustins

The Petits-Augustins Church, built in 1617, is one of the rare relics of the convent, and may be visited during exhibitions. A corridor on the left gives access to the former cloister, converted by Duban into an antique-style atrium in 1836. The Mûrier courtyard echoes with the soothing sound of water from the central fountain. The mouldings on the walls are copies of the Parthenon sculptures. To the right of the Palais des Études, in another courtyard, you can admire some arches, unfortunately rather blackened, from Hôtel de Jacques Du Faur or de Torpane, dating back to 1567.

People strolling past are generally unaware that the School of Fine Arts has a garden, and, despite the passage of time, its attraction still lies in its air of romance.

A cul-de-sac for craftsmen

50 RUE VANEAU
Métro: Vaneau or Saint-François-Xavier

High fences protect most of the numerous gardens in the 7th arrondissement from the prying eyes of passers-by. The district apparently only wants to show its austere, aloof-looking façades. However, there are some passages, not completely deserted by the crafts industry, which are more easily accessible. At 50 Rue Vaneau, not far from a school where children can be heard playing, is a charming cul-de-sac behind a small, two-storeyed house. Here, the place echoes with the sound of a large shoe-repairer's shop hard at work.

And then there was light...

THE GLASS HOUSE
31 RUE SAINT-GUILLAUME
For visits, write to the Association des Amis de la Maison de Verre (address above). Métro: Rue du Bac

Shining walls of glass, overlooking the courtyard.

The glass house in Rue Saint-Guillaume is tucked away, well out of sight, in the courtyard of an 18th-century house. Avant-garde architect Pierre Chareau, admirer of the Cubists, together with Bernard Bijvoët, built this amazing, transparent house for Dr Jean Dalsace in 1930 as a result of a constraint.

The parcel of land where Dr Dalsace planned to build his surgery and private apartment did not become available as planned. The top floor of the building on the site was occupied by an old lady who had no intention of moving! As it was impossible to demolish the building, Chareau built three, light-reflecting storeys in the space of the former ground and first floors, and left the top floor intact. The surgery is on the ground floor, while an impressive-looking, two-level reception room, a dining room, a small sitting room, and a study are on the second floor, and the bedrooms and bathrooms on the third.

The metal-latticed glass façade allows the light to flood into the house. Such transparency went against tradition because of its dismissal of the notion of inside and outside. However, this admirable house did not really set a trend, even though famous architect and city planner Le Corbusier was very impressed by it, and frequently visited the building site to make sketches of it.

The interior of the glass house is modular with sliding and pivoting panels and partitions. Chareau had an almost fanatical eye for detail, leaving nothing to chance. Even the soapdishes in the bathrooms bear the hallmark of their creator!

The Incurable

LAENNEC HOSPITAL
42 RUE DE SÈVRES
Métro: Vaneau

Well past the department store, Le Bon Marché, just where Rue de Sèvres widens, you will see an advertisement for Dubonnet, dating back to the thirties; the words "Dubo... Dubon... Dubonnet" cover the enormous gable of a six-storey building.

You are not far from the entrance to Laennec Hospital, built in the 17th and 18th centuries. Until the middle of the 19th century, it was called the Home for the Incurable – a term implying that the doctors were not really under very much pressure to get results! However, full credit must be given to the establishment for the progress made in nursing care, as it was the first in Paris to have only one patient per bed.

The originality of the hospital's architecture lies in its layout. The buildings, forming a cross, are attached to the chapel transept, thus creating eight gardens. A passage to the right of the church leads to the La Rochefoucauld courtyard, an enclosure from a bygone age with its old, iron street lamps and the 17th-century buildings rising in tiers around a circular lawn ornamented with an ancient well-curb. One of the edifices is flanked by solidly-built buttresses.

The Jules Verne arcade leads to an austere-looking chapel, where stained-glass windows used to let in the light; only a few relics of the stained-glass remain today. The most interesting item is the remarkable, 17th-century, carved, wooden pulpit, decorated with floral and religious motifs.

The La Rochefoucauld courtyard's counterpart, the Gamard courtyard (called after the architect who planned the Home for the Incurable), is on the left of the chapel, and also has a well. On one of the façades, you will see a sundial engraved by a certain Mr Boulanger in 1745.

Miracle medals from Rue du Bac

CHAPELLE DE LA MÉDAILLE-MIRACULEUSE
140 RUE DU BAC
Métro: Sèvres-Babylone

The chapel is never empty, and prayers are recited more fervently here than elsewhere. A tiny medal might work wonders.

Other relics, such the chair the Virgin Mary is said to have occupied, are on view in the chapel.

Since 1832, millions of tiny miracle medals have been struck and sold. Until recently, they were obtainable from a vending machine. A notice states that the medal should "be worn and distributed, not as a lucky charm, but with faith and love".

Was it really necessary to explain?

On November 27th, 1827, Catherine Labouré – a young country girl who had come from her native Bourgogne to join the Saint-Vincent-de-Paul Sisters of Charity – is said to have seen a vision of the Virgin Mary in the Hôtel de la Vallière chapel.

"It was half past five in the evening. In the silence following meditation, I thought I heard a noise coming from the gallery. When I looked, I caught sight of the Virgin Mary standing there, dressed for the evening, in glimmering white." Catherine was canonized in 1947.

A constant stream of pilgrims from all over the world comes to kneel for a few moments before the shrine containing Saint Catherine's remains.

Some examples of ex voto *plaques.*

Beautiful Julie...

SQUARE RÉCAMIER
AT THE END OF RUE RÉCAMIER
Métro: Sèvres-Babylone

The memory of Julie Récamier, a woman of wit and learning, and muse to Chateaubriand, lingers on in Rue Récamier where, for a long time, under the Restoration of the Bourbons, she lived and held brilliant receptions in a small apartment on the third floor, overlooking a cloistered courtyard. Men of letters such as Balzac, Musset, Hugo, Lamartine, all came to converse with this lady, whose intelligence equalled her beauty. René de Chateaubriand never failed to pay her a visit every day.

Rue Récamier was built on the site of the Abbaye-aux-Bois, demolished in 1906-7, and is now just a cul-de-sac leading to the unexpected sight of a pretty garden.

The Square, laid out on the site of Hôtel de Vaudreuil gardens (7 Rue de la Chaise) which communicated with those of Abbaye-aux-Bois, is a delightful, peaceful place with raised flowerbeds, full of all kinds of fragrant flowers – magnolias, azaleas, periwinkles – to scent the summer air.

An industrial site

23 RUE OUDINOT
Métro: Vaneau or Duroc

Despite the fact that it is named after a general of the First Empire, Rue Oudinot always looks very peaceful. There is a surprise in store for you behind the door of an ordinary-looking, 19th-century building at no. 23. Push open the door and go down the long cul-de-sac, perpendicular to Rue Oudinot.

This used to be an industrial site consisting of workshops built out of wood and brick, which have now been converted into flats. There is a fairly ordinary-looking house at the far end, past some clumps of bamboo. You will also find a few inviting benches where you can take a quiet rest in the courtyard.

A building as a billboard

BUILDINGS AT 29 AVENUE RAPP AND 3 SQUARE RAPP
Métro: École-Militaire

The building at no. 29 Avenue Rapp boasts one of the most extraordinary front doors in the city.

Architect Jules Lavirotte's Art Nouveau façades are the finest in Paris, particularly those in Avenue Rapp. Born in Lyons in 1864, he was very gifted in his use of cement, and used to call upon the services of a leading ceramics expert, Alexandre Bigot, to overlay his buildings.

It was for Bigot that Lavirotte erected the building at no. 29 in 1900. In order to please his supplier, he gave full rein to his imagination. Straight lines were abandoned in favour of entangled, extravagant curves, which, even today, never cease to amaze passers-by. This was the first time that ceramics had been used so extensively on a façade in Paris, and also an ideal opportunity to make a billboard of this six-storey building, thus advertising Bigot's work at little extra cost!

The decoration round the front door is particularly audacious. It has foliage curved round it, and is topped by two small figures which flank the face of a woman with her hair in a graceful chignon. It might even be Mrs Lavirotte's pretty face.

The entire façade is a mosaic of all sorts of surprising embellishments and motifs in brick, stone and ceramics.

Just nearby, at the far end of Square Rapp, Lavirotte put up another building, this time for himself, with a façade just as elaborately decorated.

Charming conveniences

LA MADELEINE PUBLIC TOILETS
PLACE DE LA MADELEINE
Open from 9.30 to 11.30 am and 12.30 to 18.45 pm. Métro: Madeleine

To the left of the Madeleine, near the flower market, there are some steps leading down to the most amazing underground public lavatories in the city. Unlike the extraordinarily dull-looking, coin-operated public toilets in vogue at the end of the 20th century, this "convenience" was decorated by Porcher company in an Art Nouveau style, which even experts in the genre would not have failed to recognize. The stained-glass windows of the cubicle doors are decorated with floral designs, as are the walls, and the yellows and violets add a bright, cheerful note. Each cubicle has its own washbasin. Here, we are in the ladies' area, where there used to be another room opposite, no longer in use today.

For some strange reason, in his book on public conveniences in Paris, published in 1966, Jonathan Routh failed to mention the Madeleine toilets, which must be at least four-star...

To arms!

1 RUE ROYALE
Métro: Concorde

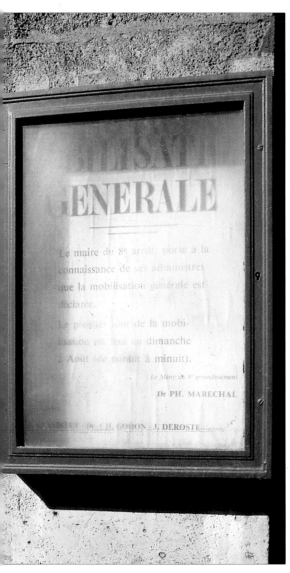

One grim day in 1914, the mayor of the 8th arrondissement put up a general mobilization notice on one of the walls of the magnificent Hôtel de Coislin. War was breaking out, and tens of thousands of Parisians were to die on the front. After mobilization, the notice should have been taken down, but those who stayed behind were so busy that they did not pay any attention to it; "Maxim's" was always full, and omnibuses crossing Place de la Concorde were being driven by women. In 1919, an observant Parisian saw the notice – a little out-of-date to say the least – and had it framed. It has been there ever since, and may even have weathered the German occupation of Paris, although it was more likely to have been a facsimile, regularly supplied by the concierge of Hôtel Coislin (now head office of a private company). Today's photocopy probably dates back to the seventies. The very presence of this flimsy piece of paper serves as a reminder of one of the bloodiest wars of the 20th century.

An air of China

LOO'S HOUSE
48 RUE DE COURCELLES
Métro: Courcelles

A red pagoda right in the heart of Paris – a rather unexpected sight – stands on the corner of Rues de Courcelles and Rembrandt. Contrary to popular belief, it was neither the former Chinese Embassy nor the traditional-style residence of a retired mandarin.

Young, well-born Mr Loo came to study in Paris at the end of the 19th century. At the age of twenty-two, he set up an oriental antiques business in Place de la Madeleine. He quickly became the leading expert in Paris, and opened up new horizons for informed collectors as well as museum curators.

In 1922, Mr Loo bought a private manor house in Rue de Courcelles, but it soon proved to be too small for his vast collections. The antique dealer then called in a French architect to build him the house of his dreams: a Chinese house in the heart of Paris.

François Bloch oversaw the building work, and the house was

finished in 1928. Mr Loo died in 1957, but C.T. Loo et Compagnie is still there.

Victims of charity

NOTRE-DAME-DE-LA-CONSOLATION CHAPEL
23 RUE JEAN-GOUJON
To visit the atrium, apply to the Italian Catholic Mission (01.42.25.61.84). Métro: Alma-Marceau

The Chapel atrium.

In 1897, some patronesses had a long wooden shed built. It housed twenty-two medieval-style booths, decorated with painted fabric and oriflammes, and topped with a canopy. Huge crowds used to pack into the shed, and they were served by 70 ladies who were the cream of Parisian high society.

A tiny, 9m by 4m booth contained an exciting attraction: the cinematograph. As a result of a mistake by the operator, the tarred shed caught fire. The flames spread rapidly, and the burning fabric suffocated many of those vainly trying to escape. There was total panic; the poor people pushed, screamed, fought, and were trampled in a frantic attempt to escape the blaze. When it was over, one hundred and twenty-five victims – including one hundred and twenty women – were retrieved from the debris.

Thanks to donations from Parisians, the bereaved families bought a plot of land where a magnificent chapel was built by architect Albert Désiré Guilbert in 1900. Squeezed between two tall buildings, the façade with its double stairway, is unusual. An inscription above the entrance ("Ne vous attristez pas comme ceux qui n'ont pas d'espérance") gives the following advice: "Don't be saddened like people without hope."

The baroque interior is Louis Quatorze, and rather interesting. A beautiful marble mosaic covers the floor. The dome, supported by four massive, grey marble columns, is ornamented with a painting by Albert Maignan. Behind the high altar, in an atrium representing the Way of the Cross, the remains of the fire victims, who died out of love for charity, are buried beneath the cenotaphs.

Little known and hardly ever visited, Notre-Dame-de-la-Consolation Chapel, a memorial to a national catastrophe, houses the Italian Catholic Mission. The building was listed in 1980.

A royal smile

SQUARE LOUIS XVI, CHAPEL OF ATONEMENT

Open on Wednesdays only, from 9.30 or 10 am to 1 pm, and 2 pm to 4/5 or 6 pm, depending on the time of year. Group visits: 01.48.09.83.54/01.48.20.15.57. Métro: Saint-Augustin

In Square Louis XVI stands a chapel of atonement, erected on the site of the cemetery, where those guillotined at the Concorde were buried. The remains of Louis XVI and Marie-Antoinette were also laid to rest here. In 1794, the cemetery was closed and sold by lots at low prices. However, after spotting the royal tombs, a royalist neighbour bought back the site, and gave it to Louis XVIII. Excavations took place, and the king's remains, as well as those of Marie-Antoinette, whose stockings worn on the day of her execution helped identify her, were disinterred. Chateaubriand made the macabre claim that she had been recognized because of her smile. The monarchs' ashes were transferred to the Saint-Denis Basilica where they remain today. Between 1816 and 1826, architect Fontaine erected this neoclassical edifice on the ground of the original cemetery. The chapel is ornamented with sculptures by J. B. Plantar and bas-relief sculptures by A. F. Gérard. A group by Bosio shows Louis XVI looking up at the sky, and *Marie-Antoinette* is by Cortot. The tombs in the courtyard are in memory of the Swiss Guards who fell when the Tuileries Palace was attacked on August 10th, 1792.

"By appointment to the Emperor"

CITÉ ODIOT
26 RUE DE WASHINGTON
Métro: George-V

Cité Odiot, overlooking the garden.

Long, narrow passages off Rue Washington lead to Cité Odiot, an oasis in the busy Champs-Élysées area. This long block of buildings, shadowed by beautiful trees, was built in 1847. It was named after goldsmith Jean-Baptiste Odiot, born in 1763, who had a superb, luxurious private residence built here for his own use. All that remains of that harmoniously-designed group of buildings are the stables.

After a long period of decline during the French Revolution and the ensuing Reign of Terror, the goldsmith's trade picked up again.

Odiot made a fortune, and bought a domain in the Nièvre and a manor house on the corner of Quai d'Orsay and Rue du Bac. After receiving the Gold Medal at the third Industrial Exhibition in 1801, Odiot's name became associated with the Empire, and orders started pouring in. This prestigious company made the imperial sceptre and sword for Napoleon I, who later ordered a cradle for his son, Napoleon II, king of Rome.

In 1814, alongside the valiant soldiers pushing back the Russian and Prussian troops, the goldsmith volunteered, as Colonel of the National Guard, to defend the Clichy tollgate.

In 1824, Odiot made his home in Rue de l'Oratoire (now Rue de Washington), where he held sumptuous soirees before settling down to a quieter life, growing orange trees and playing billiards.

An islet of Romantics

THE ROMANTICS MUSEUM, 16 RUE CHAPTAL
Open to the public every day except Mondays from 10 am to 5.40 pm. Tel: 01.48.74.95.38.
Métro: Blanche

A long, tree-lined passage opens out into a delightful, paved courtyard where the air is fragrant with the scent of roses and seringas. The pretty, one-storeyed house was built on the site of the former Tivoli gardens in 1820. In 1830, Dutch painter Ary Scheffer moved in and lived there for thirty years. Every Friday evening, he would entertain his literary and artistic friends – Gobineau, Ingres, Béranger, Delacroix, Turgenev, Liszt, Lamennais, Renan, the cream of the Romantic Movement in Paris.

In 1856, Ernest Renan, author of *La Vie de Jésus* (The Life of Jesus) married Cornélie, Ary Scheffer's niece. Renan's great-granddaughter sold the house to the State in 1956, keeping the atelier for her own use.

Today, the Romantics Museum is an extension of the Carnavalet Museum. Moving mementoes of novelist George Sand have found an excellent home in these leafy surroundings, miraculously sheltered from the tumult of city life. Items concerning the life of the Marshal of Saxony under the reign of Louis XV recall the strong personality of the writer's great-grandfather.

Recently, Ary Scheffer's atelier was reconstructed with meticulous attention to detail, and added to the

The museum's spick and span façade.

museum. You will appreciate the tiny winter garden and rockery, where you can take a quiet rest. In 19th-century Paris, there were many peaceful, secluded, green spaces like this one, just right for work and meditation.

Housing for workers

CITÉ NAPOLÉON
58 RUE ROCHECHOUART
Métro: Anvers

Cité Napoléon, a haven of peace in the heart of the bustling Rochechouart district.

An ordinary, Italian-style block of flats, seen from the street, belies the unexpected presence of an attractive, Louis Napoleon housing development. It is the sole evidence of what was originally a vast undertaking to build a cooperative with individual flats and communal areas for four hundred working families in each district. To this end, an association was formed, and Louis Napoleon donated 500,000 francs in order to convince the people of the social nature of his election.

Built between 1849 and 1853, the development was intended mainly for the neighbouring gasworks employees. There were 86 apartments in the first building;

rooms without heating cost 100 francs, those with heating, 150 francs. An inspector was appointed to keep an eye on the inhabitants' behaviour, and the gates were closed at ten in the evening. The doctor visited the tenants free of charge, and there were communal wash houses, drying rooms and bathrooms. The Napoleon housing development, a veritable "cité radieuse" – Le Corbusier's "living unit", built in Marseilles (1947-52) – before its time, was typical of the fashion for Fourierist theories during the last century.

However, such indulgence towards the underprivileged was not without ulterior motives. In 1857, on the eve of the elections, the estate manager put up the following notice: "Tenants, I would be failing in my duty if I did not remind you that it is owing to His Majesty the Emperor's great concern for the welfare of the working classes as a whole and of yours in particular, and thanks to immense sacrifices, that you have received such benefits. Thus, in view of the above-mentioned and because of the good relations I have always had with you, I hereby request you to go to the polls on Sunday and prove your gratitude to the Emperor by voting for his candidate."

Housing for artists

SQUARE D'ORLÉANS
80 RUE TAITBOUT
Métro: Trinité

Square d'Orléans is one of the main highlights of the Nouvelle Athènes district, frequented by artists, musicians, actors, dancers, singers, and writers. To reach it, go down a high-ceilinged, heavily ornamented passage, cross one courtyard, and you will come into another, bigger courtyard with a fountain in the middle.

It was in 1830 that English architect Edward Crecy designed and built Square d'Orléans on the site of the former domain of *Comédie-Française* actress Mademoiselle Mars. Another Englishman, barrister Edward Richardson, whose great passion was ancient architecture, bought the Square, made a few alterations, and installed the fountain.

The British architects' preference for bricks, along with their style of building, endows the Square with a genre which distinguishes it from other 19th-century private housing developments in Paris.

Right from the start, it was a place of luxury, frequented by artistic and literary celebrities. Novelist George Sand moved into no. 85 in 1842, and Chopin lived at no. 9. Alexandre Dumas *père*, another resident here, gave a memorable party in his apartment decorated by Jadin, Delacroix, Boulanger, Grandville and Nanteuil. Many others decided to take up residence in this community of the Arts: opera singer Pauline Viardot, ballet dancer Marie Taglioni, painter and caricaturist Dantan Jeune, and pianist Zimmermann who used to entertain his neighbour, Chopin, as well as Liszt, Rossini and Berlioz, in his music room.

Silence reigns in Square d'Orléans today, but with the help of a little imagination, you might hear a few notes of music coming from the windows!

Thérèse, queen of Paris

DOSNE-THIERS LIBRARY AND HÔTEL DE LA PAÏVA
27 AND 28 PLACE SAINT-GEORGES
Métro: Saint-Georges

There is a lovely fountain in the middle of Place Saint-George, around which generations of car drivers and bus drivers have circled. However, the place looked quite different in 1840 when speculators of the Saint Georges Company decided to create a circular space designed to become the focal point of the "new Saint-Georges district".

The Dosne-Thiers library with its sedate-looking façade stands at no. 27. Speculator Dosne's wife was the first to have a house built on this site. In 1833, she sold it to French statesman and historian Adolphe Thiers, to whom she also offered her daughter's hand in marriage. Thiers lived here with his wife, his mother-in-law and his sister-in-law, and did most of his work in his study-cum-library on the second floor. His magnificent art collection, including his porcelain from China, was saved *in extremis* by the painter Courbet during the Paris Commune of 1871. However, he was unable to prevent the house from being burned down. The rebuilding of the house you see today was funded by the State in 1873.

Opposite, on the other side of the Place, at no. 28, you will notice a fine neo-Renaissance building, whose heavy decorations caused a scandal when it was erected in 1840. Architect Renaud's intention was to compensate the narrowness of the façade by lavishly ornamenting it with cherubs, griffins and lions. At first-floor level stand figures representing Architecture (with its ruler), Sculpture (with its hammer), Wisdom and Abundance. A certain Thérèse Lachmann took up residence on the ground floor, and her salon became a must for celebrities of Parisian elite society. A wealthy Portuguese, the Marquis de Païva, succeeded in attracting the pretty young woman's attention, and married her. She became known as "the Païva" and reigned over Parisian society. She had a manor house built on the Champs-Élysées, lived the good life, and became one of the most famous courtesans of the Second Empire.

*Left: **The Dosne-Thiers library.***
*Above: **The façade of Hôtel de la Païva.***

Atmosphere...

HÔTEL DU NORD
102 QUAI DE JEMMAPES
Métro: Gare de l'Est

Saint-Martin canal, built between 1822 and 1825, with nine locks, five bridges, five footbridges and three swing bridges, offers one of the most poetic strolls in Paris.

Hôtel du Nord on Quai de Jemmapes has come to symbolize both a mythical version of Paris and a film, and is a place of pilgrimage for cinema enthusiasts. In 1929, Eugène Dabit, the hotel owners' son, published a collection of short stories depicting the lives of hotel-keepers and their clients. Shortly after his death in 1936, French film director Marcel Carné was inspired by the book to make his famous film, *Hôtel du Nord*. Film set designer Alexandre Trauner recreated the hotel surroundings in Boulogne-Billancourt studios. Only a few scenes were shot outside, near the footbridge, for the purpose of continuity. The film, released in December 1938, was a great success, and the general public became acquainted with the canal, already described by Marius Richard in 1935: "Who has never walked along these black and white banks, one for the coal which blackens mens' faces and the other for the limestone which whitens them? Who has never strolled alongside, and run their fingers over, the tarred wooden barges, which, when unloaded, stand high in the water? [...] They form a floating village, and the sight of it waking up in the morning, preferably in the summer, as the keeper unhurriedly opens the gates of the Bassin de la Villette, should not be missed. A dog barks, a bargeman looks out of his cabin, the water laps along the brown hulls, seasoned like old pipes; pigeons coo, a woman chops wood, another stands with her arms folded while waiting for the water for the coffee to boil; the decks are being washed, breakfast is ready..."

In 1984, an association foiled part of a plan to demolish the hotel. Its president was the actress Arletty, who starred as a prostitute in Carné's film, and was famous for the catch phrase, "Atmosphere, atmosphere...". However, only the façade of the hotel was saved, an empty shell looking like a film set. The ground-floor restaurant, decorated by a film-set designer in the style of the period, serves traditional food, and a band plays music in the evenings.

An abandoned convent

THE FORMER CONVENT OF THE RECOLLECTS
SQUARE VILLEMIN – 8 RUE DES RÉCOLLETS/148 RUE DU FAUBOURG-SAINT-MARTIN
Métro: Gare de l'Est

S ome of the Recollects' convent buildings are still standing in the Villemin public garden opposite Gare de l'Est. The Recollects, reformed Franciscan monks under the protection of Henry IV and Marie de Médicis (she laid the cornerstone of their church), came here in 1603. The convent buildings were erected in 1619.

The convent prospered rapidly, and became particularly well-known for its library of 30,000 volumes, its works of art and its collection of curios. The monks were driven out during the French Revolution, and the place was used for various purposes, especially military, which brought about extensive changes.

The stones reveal the passing of several eras. The buildings, in disrepair and supported by struts on the Rue du Faubourg-Saint-Martin side, date back to the 16th century. The interior of the 17th-century, pinnacled chapel is in ruins, and cannot be visited. However, the façade of a fine, well-preserved, sedate-looking, three-storeyed building, over almost one hundred metres long, and dating back to the

The unadorned façade of the former convent spans over almost a hundred metres.

18th century, can be seen from the garden. It has no ornamentations save a pediment and a medallion framed by decorative keystones on the slightly projecting part of the façade, and according to a clock set in the pediment triangle on a background of sculpted foliage, it is always twenty-five to six.

As the result of an association's fairly recent actions, the Square has been considerably extended on the Saint-Martin canal side. Square Villemin is a very pleasant green space, a rare sight in this highly built-up area. Hopefully, the remains of the convent buildings will soon be restored.

Such a tiny house!

39 RUE DU CHÂTEAU-D'EAU
Métro: République

Very little is known about the smallest house in Paris, barely noticeable, wedged between two tall buildings. This funny little place, about the size of a doll's house (approximately 1.20m wide and 5m high), comprises a ground-floor workshop and one upstairs room, and is alleged to have been built as the result of a family quarrel. The former site of the house used to be a passage linking Rue du Château-d'Eau and Rue du Faubourg-Saint-Martin. However, since the heirs to the land were unable to reach an agreement, the owner simply blocked up the tiny alley by erecting this tiny house, an unequivocal answer to the problem!

The city has some other "records" that deserve special mention. The shortest street in the capital, Rue des Degrés in the 2nd arrondissement, measures 5.75m long, and is, in fact, a set of fourteen steps between Rue Beauregard and Rue de Cléry. The longest street, Rue de Vaugirard (4,360m), starts at Boulevard Saint-Michel, goes through the 6th and 15th arrondissements, and ends at Boulevards Victor and Lefebvre. The narrowest street, Rue de Venise (4th arrondissement), is 2m wide, with Rue du Chat-qui-Pêche (5th arrondissement), a close second, measuring 2.50m.

In quarantine

SAINT-LOUIS HOSPITAL
2 PLACE DU DOCTEUR-ALFRED-FOURNIER
Please note that the historic Saint-Louis quadrangle is closed at weekends. Métro: Goncourt

The central courtyard of Saint-Louis Hospital is very impressive, and, with its green lawns surrounded by tall stone and brick buildings, is somewhat reminiscent of Place des Vosges in the 3rd arrondissement (without the arcades, of course). This peaceful quadrangle, planted with trees, has hardly changed since the 17th century.

When there were widespread epidemics, it was the custom to isolate the sick outside the city in order to reduce the risk of contagion. In the 16th century, health inspectors assembled the plague victims in tents, away from the city centre. Henry IV (known as Henry of Navarre), who had ambitious plans for the architecture of Paris, decided to create a royal nursing home in the early 17th century. This hospital, a veritable fortress designed to prevent the spread of disease, was surrounded by a wall. Vegetable gardens and orchards within the enclosure made it self-sufficient. An L-shaped group of four buildings, housing staff and administration, formed another barrier. The central quadrangle was reserved for patients only. They stayed on the first floor for a long time, while the vaulted ground floor areas were used to store grain. Only the chapel, still standing, was built in front of the walls to make it available to the congregation outside the hospital.

In 1818, Philippe Lebon built France's first gasworks next to the chapel. Gas pipes were made out of 1,500 gun tubes provided by the War Ministry, and, on December 25th, 1819, Parisians celebrated the first midnight Mass to take place in a chapel with such modern lighting.

A prosperous nursing home

DR BELHOMME'S HOME
157-61 RUE DE CHARONNE
Métro: Alexandre-Dumas

Behind some tall buildings stand three attractive houses, looking out onto a pleasant garden. The middle, most recently-built, house is ornamented with garlands, cartouches, and lions' heads; the other two have a flight of steps each. This is all that remains of "Pension Belhomme", a nursing home for the insane founded by former carpenter Jacques Belhomme in 1768; the rest was demolished in 1972.

Accommodation and treatment were not free, so that only those from well-to-do families were accepted as inmates. The business really came into its own during the Reign of Terror, when the Jacobins' opponents were systematically executed during the French Revolution. The home not only provided the inmates with excellent treatment, it also protected those wishing to escape the Revolutionary Tribunal and the guillotine; the Duchess of Orleans spent a long time there.

Belhomme would appear to have had no qualms about profiting from such a situation! The Duchess of Choiseul, unable to pay her way, is alleged to have been thrown out – and guillotined shortly afterwards.

Imprisoned on January 28th, 1794, and condemned for misappropriation of public funds, Belhomme was reinstated a few months later as manager of his nursing home.

Workshops and dormitories for craftsmen

RUE DES IMMEUBLES-INDUSTRIELS
Métro: Nation

The tall buildings lining Rue des Immeubles-Industriels, between Boulevard Voltaire and Rue du Faubourg-Saint-Antoine, are rather unusual with their slender cast-iron columns, and are evidence of some of the industrial achievements of the 19th century. Industrialist Jean-François Cail, who instigated this project for the good of the community, had the inspired idea of providing the craftsmen and their families with modern workshops and decent accommodation under the same roof.

Work on the nineteen buildings began in 1872 under the supervision of architect Émile Leménil, and was completed a year later. The workshops on the ground floor, the mezzanine, and the first floor were occupied by craftsmen mainly connected with the furniture trade, and the accommodation on the upper floors was fitted out with basic home comforts such as water, light, gas and space. Power was supplied by an enormous 200 hp steam engine, manufactured by Cail et Compagnie, and installed under the road.

In the late 19th century, two thousand people were working and living in Rue des Immeubles-Industriels.

The flagstones of death

THE SITE OF THE GUILLOTINE
16 RUE DE LA CROIX-FAUBIN
Métro: Voltaire

Men sentenced to death were kept in the Grande-Roquette prison, built in 1836. It used to stand on the site of nos. 164-68 Rue de la Roquette, and was demolished in 1899. Five granite flagstones embedded in the ground on the corner of Rue de la Croix-Faubin serve as a reminder of the times when the guillotine was routinely set up in front of the prison; five regrettably famous flagstones, about which Aristide Briand wrote songs, as did Pierre François Lacenaire, murderer and a man of letters:

"Oh, I know you well,
footholds for a scaffold;
Immaculate white stones,
bearing no signs
of the executioner's bloody deeds."

The prison got its nickname – Abbey of the Five Stones – from the flagstones used by the executioner's assistants to securely wedge into place the sinister uprights of the guillotine, thus ensuring that the blade slid straight down to the lunette. Although executions took place at night only, they never failed to attract crowds of bystanders who were only too pleased to watch.

On the other side of Rue de la Roquette stood the Petite-Roquette prison, built between 1826 and 1830, which became a prison for women in 1835. In 1974, it was demolished, and public gardens, Square de la Petite-Roquette, were laid out on the site. All that remains of the former prison is the porch, which is now the entrance to the gardens.

Flying…

11, 13, 15 Rue Titon
Métro: Faidherbe-Chaligny

Opposite an unusual-looking Lutheran church, at nos. 11, 13 and 15, out of sight behind a long, five-storeyed building are three attractive courtyards dating back to the late 19th century. The building's wooden framework is reinforced with pieces of metal, decorated with strange-looking lions' heads.

Rue Titon extends over the site of an extravagantly majestic manor house built in 1673 by the son of a skilled, self-employed embroiderer from the Saint-Antoine faubourg, Maximilien Titon, who made a fortune selling arms. Mockingly nicknamed "Titonville", this splendid property comprised eight houses, built side by side, with five doors opening out onto Rue des Boulets and Rue de Montreuil. A six-columned portico used to give access to a formal garden, ornamented with pools and statues. Maximilien's son, intensely loyal to Louis XIV, wished to erect an immense, sixty-foot-high statue in his honour. Sculptor Louis Garnier, pupil of Girardon (who created many of the sculptures at Versailles), worked ten years on the project which was never completed.

In 1763, Jean-Baptiste Réveillon set up his wallpaper factory on the site of Hôtel Titon's outbuildings. Twenty years later, in 1783, he lent the

premises to physicist Pilâtre de Rozier who built the first hot air balloon there, out of canvas and paper; it went up on October 19th of the same year. This was the start of aeronautical exploits – already experienced by the tragic Greek mythic figure of Icarus – which were to make man's wildest dreams come true: flying.

Artisans' alley

186 Rue de la Roquette
Métro: Philippe-Auguste

Near the top of Rue de la Roquette, not far from Père Lachaise cemetery, some artisans' workshops, surrounded by blocks of modern buildings, have stood the test of time. This U-shaped group of two-storeyed, brick buildings, converted and renovated, now houses offices on the ground floor. A few flowers are all that is needed to brighten up this surprising little alley, vaguely reminiscent of the areas where the craft industries used to flourish on the east side of Paris.

A cock and some primroses

COUR DU COQ
60 RUE SAINT-SABIN
Métro: Chemin-Vert

Cour du Coq, near Rue du Faubourg-Saint-Antoine, is a quiet, obscure, paved cul-de-sac, preserved and very well looked after. It stretches out a long way behind a beautiful green gate decorated, not surprisingly, with a proud-looking cock, and has a gutter all the way down the middle to drain off rainwater not caught by the numerous pots of flowers dotted about.

The names of neighbouring cul-de-sacs at nos. 50 and 58 – Impasse des Primevères (Primrose Street) and Allée Verte (Green Street) – recall the district's rural past, when Rue Saint-Sabin ran alongside the counterscarp of the city's fortifications.

Stardust in the Faubourg

COUR DE L'ÉTOILE-D'OR
75 RUE DU FAUBOURG-SAINT-ANTOINE
Métro: Bastille

The 18th-century sundial in Cour de l'Étoile-d'Or.

A very pleasant way of spending a sunny day is to walk down Rue du Faubourg-Saint-Antoine, and chance upon a series of courtyards reminiscent of the times when the air smelt of glue and sanded wood. Intended as homes for well-to-do Parisians, now and in the future, the workshops in these courtyards are being vacated for renovation purposes. In the past, visitors to the Faubourg were greeted by the sound of hammers tapping on and planes smoothing down planks of rare wood; partly-finished furniture would be lined up outside, and French-polished armchairs would be hanging on hooks to dry.

All that remains today is the architecture of those courtyards, recalling the not too distant past when the Faubourg was still surrounded by countryside.

No. 75 opens into the Cour de l'Étoile-d'Or (Golden Star), which dates back to the second half of the 17th century, although its name only goes back to the late 18th century. One building, near a trompe l'oeil recalling the Faubourg's activities, stands out: a small, greyish house, built across the passage. This beautiful old house, once two storeys high, is in an advanced state of disrepair.

There is a sundial on the front wall engraved by a certain Mr Sevin in 1751. Inside, there is a remarkable, wooden, balustraded, 17th-century staircase with carved figures representing the seasons. Originally, it was a 17th-century country cottage belonging to Jacques Moncel du Vivien. In 1700, Jacques La Rocque moved in, converted the garden into a courtyard for artisans, and rented small buildings to cabinetmakers. Hangars and stables were added, and another owner, Nicolas Defaux, took over in 1782.

In the first courtyard, on the right, there is a small, colourful, 18th-century house, renovated under the First Empire.

In the second courtyard stand early 19th-century buildings, along with another edifice put up by architect Chabot on the former site of the stables in 1882.

When you enter other courtyards dotted along Rue du Faubourg-Saint-Antoine, and despite the alterations and the current use made of former cabinetmakers' workshops, you cannot fail to take a step back in time: the 17th-century courtyard at no. 33 with a well behind a house and a balustraded staircase under a beamed passageway, all of the same period; Cour des Trois-Frères (nos. 81-3); Cour de la Maison-Brûlée (no. 89); Cour de l'Ours (no. 95), whose sign still decorates the façade, and which, on the right-hand side of the entrance to a small building, has a thin, *Directoire* door with palm-leaf mouldings; Cour du Saint-Esprit (no. 127); Passage de la Main-d'Or (no. 133). And the list does not stop there. Here, more than in any other arrondissement, you should not hesitate to push open doors – fortunately not all fitted with entry code systems.

January to June...

PASSAGE DU CHEVAL-BLANC
2 RUE DE LA ROQUETTE
Métro: Bastille

Passage du Cheval-Blanc is reached through a late 17th-century building. Originally devoted to the craft industry, this is one of those places which are being renovated and converted into "trendy" apartments. At the end of the passage, a bend leads to the building on Rue du Faubourg-Saint-Antoine (nos. 19-20), called Cité Parchappe after the Parchappe family who used to live here and who, in the 19th century, undertook a great deal of alteration work. In the early 20th century, the passage began to look as it does today. It will take you from January to June to walk along this passage – a succession of very dissimilar courtyards named after the first few months of the year!

Mid-19th-century buildings stand in Janvier courtyard. In Février and Mars courtyards, timbered workshops stretch out behind a more recent building. Avril is not a courtyard, but a three-storeyed building, while Mai courtyard was rebuilt by architect Sauger in 1910. Juin courtyard is lined with timbered buildings. Some artisans can still be seen at work in Passage du Cheval-Blanc, which, for a long time, was the site of numerous timber warehouses in the Faubourg, the district of cabinetmakers and furniture makers in general.

A passage in the Faubourg

PASSAGE LHOMME
26 RUE DE CHARONNE
Métro: Ledru-Rollin

Before Avenue Ledru-Rollin was built, there used to be a network of dark, narrow little streets leading to Rue de Charonne. One of these, Passage Lhomme, is reminiscent of the bygone days of the Faubourg, where the workers were legion and hard at work in the busy workshops smelling of sawdust, glue and varnish. Today, all that remains are the Remlinger mirror factory established

in 1886, French polisher Hollard established in 1912, and offices which have replaced the old workshops.

The paving stones are old and pitted, and there are lots of vines growing up the walls of the three- and four-storeyed buildings lining Passage Lhomme, which, a little congested with cars, runs through an 18th-century building into Rue de Charonne.

Convents in the country

NOTRE-DAME-DE-BON-SECOURS AND LA MADELEINE DE TRESNEL
99-101 RUE DE CHARONNE (CITÉ DU COUVENT) AND 100 RUE DE CHARONNE
Métro: Alexandre-Dumas

beautiful neoclassical convent chapel in 1937, and its portal in 1969, some of convent buildings have survived, and can be seen at no. 99. A large, rectangular courtyard leads to a smaller courtyard, both of which are surrounded by similar-looking buildings erected by Nicolas d'Orbay in 1739, and to which storeys were added in the 19th century.

The religious calling of the Bon-Secours Convent suffered a great deal during the French Revolution, and the buildings were converted into a cotton spinning factory in the early 19th century. Later still, they housed a school of industrial arts and commerce, and then a hospice.

Opposite, at no. 10, in the early 18th century, another renowned convent, La Madeleine de Tresnel, had gardens stretching as far as present-day Rue Léon-Frot and Rue de Montreuil. The convent buildings were erected around two courtyards and a chapel with a round church tower. The remains of La Madeleine de Tresnel Convent – some of the arches on the side overlooking the street, the old church tower, and a few buildings – cannot be visited today as plans are being made to build offices, apartments and shops, according to the company owning the premises.

R ue de Charonne follows the route of one of the oldest roads in Paris, which used to link Charonne village to the capital. It was here, in the country, that many religious orders were established during the 17th century. The Bon-Secours nuns settled in Rue de Charonne in 1648. Despite the unfortunate demolition of the

Buddha under the trees

BOIS DE VINCENNES BUDDHIST CENTRE
40 ROUTE DE CEINTURE DU LAC DAUMESNIL
For visits, phone 01.43.41.54.48. Métro: Porte Dorée

Buddhist Centre in the heart of the woods.

A group sculpture by Japanese artist Torao Yazaki graces the entrance to the Bois de Vincennes Buddhist Centre. The French Togo and Cameroun pavilions, where we are now, were designed by architects Louis-Hippolyte Boileau and Léon Carrière for the Colonial Exhibition in 1931. For a time, the bigger pavilion housed a museum devoted to the timber industries, and, as a result of this temporary occupancy, was fitted with pinewood roofing.

In 1977, it was decided to dedicate the place entirely to Buddha, which is confirmed by the presence of an imposing statue of "The Enlightened One" inside the building. The Tibetan Temple, built in 1985 according to spiritual leader Kalu Rinpoche's instructions, stands nearby. The symbolic elements of the edifice will probably mean little to those unfamiliar with the religion, but there can be no doubt that they convey infinite wisdom. For instance, the canopy above the porch would appear to express the primacy of spiritual matters over temporal ones... a truth which one cannot help but meditate upon throughout the visit.

Houses by the Seine

RUE CRÉMIEUX
Métro: Gare de Lyon

Rue Crémieux, near Gare de Lyon, is the picturesque site of a small, 19th-century housing development for workers. At first, it was called the Millaud development, which was marked out in 1857, and built almost as a single block. The merits of the houses – 35 in all and two-storeyed at the most – were praised in a newspaper article written at the time: "Each house comprises a basement kitchen, and a total of six rooms, with heating, on the ground floor and the two upper storeys.

There are no concierges, and you can be master in your own home for a yearly rent of seven hundred francs."

The street was pedestrianized in 1993. Some of the façades have been renovated, and the road, repaved. Old-fashioned streetlamps give this quiet little street an air reminiscent of bygone days. A small faience plaque at no. 8 indicates the level of the water – 1.75 metres – in Rue Crémieux when the Seine overflowed its banks on January 28 and 29th, 1910!

The Black Musketeers' gaming table

COUR DU BEL-AIR
56 RUE DU FAUBOURG-SAINT-ANTOINE
Métro: Bastille

The furniture makers, cabinetmakers, upholsterers, French-polishers and japanners who used to occupy the courtyards and side streets of Rue du Faubourg-Saint-Antoine at the beginning of the century are not easy to find nowadays.

The entrance to Cour du Bel-Air is on the former site of a manor house of the same name. A long corridor, whose exposed beams hold up nothing but air, leads to two smaller courtyards, both surrounded by three-storeyed buildings. Here, as in many of the Faubourg's courtyards, there are vines everywhere, and grapes brush against the heads of passers-by.

In the first courtyard, opposite an attractive, green-coloured, Gothic Revival shop near the middle, one of the paving stones is bigger than the rest. Legend has it that the Black Musketeers from the neighbouring barracks used it as a gaming table. In fact, there used to be some very old wooden steps here, known for a long time as the "musketeers' staircase."

The last wash house

THE LENOIR MARKET WASH HOUSE
3 RUE DE COTTE
Métro: Ledru-Rollin

300 of these establishments, whose friendly, rough and ready, quarrelsome clients created an atmosphere often described by novelist Emile Zola.

The Rue de Cotte wash house made its entry into literature on December 3rd, 1851, when Victor Hugo's cab tried to reach a barricade in Faubourg Saint-Antoine during the 1851 coup d'état. The writer recounts the scene in his book, *Histoire d'un crime* (Story of a Crime):

"Which way do we go, sir?"
"Towards the sound of the guns firing."
We were in a narrow street; on my left I could see the words, GRAND LAVOIR, inscribed over the doorway, and on my right, a square with a building in the middle, resembling an indoor market. The square and the street were deserted; I asked the coachman:
"What street are we in?"
"Rue de Cotte."
"Where is the Roysin café?"
"Straight ahead."
"Let's go there."

Place d'Aligre, generally rather dull and bleak, brightens up on Sundays thanks to a lively, bustling market. The outline of one of finest indoor markets in Paris – "Beauveau", built in 1843 by Marc-Gabriel Jolivet to replace an 18th-century building – can be made out at the far end.

Without the determination of residents in the district, the façade of the "grand lavoir du marché Lenoir" would have disappeared. This small, pedimented wash house used to stand at 9 Rue de Cotte (it has kept its number) before being moved 40 metres down the road to make room for the building of community facilities.

The Aligre wash house was built in 1830, and is the only one of its kind in Paris. There used to be around

The Star-Spangled Banner flying at Picpus

PICPUS CEMETERY, 35 RUE DE PICPUS
Open every day at 2.30 pm except Sundays and Mondays. Tel: 01.43.44.18.54. Métro: Nation

From June 14th to July 27th, 1794 (during the Reign of Terror when those brought before the Revolutionary Tribunal were systematically executed), bloodstained carts shuttled back and forth between the guillotine on Place de la Nation and a rectangular, hastily-dug grave in a field near the disused convent of Augustinian canonesses. These grim trips lasted seven weeks: 1,306 people were beheaded and "escorted" to Picpus, a place originally intended for a more light-hearted purpose.

A certain Mr Coignard's plans to establish a convalescent home there came to halt when the garden was requisitioned and converted into a mass grave. Despite residents' protests, a wall was knocked down to enable the carts to get through more easily. The site was located at the far end of a plot of land so as to avoid attracting attention.

This was the final resting place of the cream of the aristocracy as well as of minor nobility and a great many

General La Fayette' s tombstone.

commoners, 702 to be exact. The land fell into disuse, and, in 1802, was bought up by families of those who were guillotined. Even today, only descendants of the victims can claim to be buried at Picpus.

General de La Fayette was interred there next to his wife, Marie-Adrienne de Noailles, whose family was almost entirely wiped out during the Reign of Terror. The American national colours pay tribute to the heroes of the US War of Independence, undoubtedly the only American flag to fly in Paris without a break since 1834, including the years of the German occupation.

Just like Puss in Boots

THE GREEN BASTILLE-VINCENNES PROMENADE
VARIOUS ACCESS POINTS ALONG AVENUE DAUMESNIL
Métro: Ledru-Rollin, Dugommier or Daumesnil

Few green spaces are being created in Paris these days, although some continue to make a miraculous appearance in the heart of this increasingly concrete-bound city. Thanks to the Bastille-Vincennes Promenade, dreams of a walk through the city, away from the noise, the smoke and, above all, the traffic, can now come true.

It is divided into two sections: the Viaduct of the Arts and the tree-lined Esplanade. It begins just after the interior design shops near the Bastille Opera House, and follows the route of a former railway which used to operate on Sundays, taking Parisians to the Bois de Vincennes or to the open-air cafés along the river Marne. Go up the steps at the corner of Avenue Ledru-Rollin and Avenue Daumesnil. The vast arches of the viaduct used to house workshops,

and are now the home of Arts and Crafts' activities. At the top, you will find a grass-edged, asphalt path, lined with lime trees. The view over the surrounding buildings turns the walk into a veritable jaunt over the rooftops. First of all, there is a garden parallel to the esplanade, planted with maple trees and ornamented with small fountains. Further along, the esplanade then overlooks a brick terrace and, further down still, some trees in Square Hector-Malet, which was created in 1994. After narrowing a little between two newly-erected buildings, the path widens and has an ornamental pool all the way down the centre. You are now in Rue Jacques-Hillairet which runs through a newly-developed area. With the help of a wooden footbridge, you can "jump over" Reuilly Garden and its circular lawn, just as Puss in Boots might have done. On your right, you can see the former Reuilly train station, preserved and restored. This is where the viaduct ends, and the tree-lined Esplanade begins. There are two tunnels. The first starts between two embankments planted with cherry trees, near a cycle path, and comes out at Rue Sibuet. You can then continue your walk under Boulevard Soult right up to Boulevard de la Guyane.

Time stands still

RUE DE REUILLY
Métro: Faidherbe-Chaligny

Formerly a medieval path, Rue de Reuilly, now lined with unsightly buildings, has undergone many changes. Who would have thought that attractive, picturesque cul-de-sacs could be found here? And yet, they can!

At no. 18, a passage closed by metal gate leads to a delightful little courtyard. Each house in this tiny cul-de-sac, built in the late 19th century, has its own stairway. Small zinc awnings and, above all, the house at the far end, topped by a lantern, give the place an indefinable appeal. The clock is a trompe l'oeil painting, where time stands still at seven minutes past five. The walls

and part of the passage are overrun with vines.

As you come out, cross over to the other side of Rue de Reuilly. Thanks to a discerning property developer, the house at no. 29 was restored, and one-storeyed buildings erected to form a small cul-de-sac, which, decorated with a few flowers, has an atmosphere all of its own.

After the crossroads at Boulevard Diderot, Impasse Mousset starts at 83 Rue de Reuilly, and is surprisingly long. Its workshops and small offices are still in business. Halfway down, an old rusty sign smothered in wisteria is a reminder that a hotel-cum-bar used to stand here.

Finally, no. 67 is the opulent-looking entrance to Cour Alsace-Lorraine. No greenery here. The courtyard is divided into two cul-de-sacs. The one on the left has a wooden stairway of a type rarely to be found in Paris today, while that on the right leads to a big garden surrounding a beautiful, mysterious-looking house.

Bastion no. 1

BOULEVARD PONIATOWSKI (NEAR RUE ROBERT-ETLIN)
Métro: Porte de Charenton

Over the centuries, walls have been built around Paris in order to protect the city. The last one was known as the Thiers (first president of the Third Republic from 1871 to 1873) wall, because the decision to build new fortifications was made during Thiers' term of office as Minister of War. Building work started in 1841, and lasted four years. The end result was a wall – 34 metres long, 142 metres wide, with 94 bastions – surrounding not only the city of Paris itself but also its immediate suburbs. However, the actual strategic significance of these fortifications was never really established, and they were almost totally demolished in 1929.

Apartment blocks were built on the site, including the area where building was prohibited, and a few – rare – green spaces were laid out.

Bastion no. 44 (Porte de Clichy) and bastion no. 1 are the last remaining bastions. A paved avenue gently slopes from Boulevard Poniatowski towards bastion no. 1, polygonal-shaped and a few hundred metres long, topped by a casemate with loopholes. From the top of bastion, there is a good view over the Seine – and the incessant flow of traffic heading towards the motorway. Near the circular road, there are some remains of the curtain wall, 4 to 5 metres high, which used to run between the bastions.

Paris ends here

PARIS BOUNDARY MARKER
304 RUE DE CHARENTON
Métro: Dugommier

The marble plaque on the wall (see photo) bears the following inscription: "1726. Boundary markers. Under the reign of Louis XV. By order of the King. Building strictly prohibited between these boundary markers and the next village, a punishable offence according to His Majesty's declarations of 1724 (and) 1726." Louis XV was the great-grandson of Louis XIV, and was known as the "Well-Beloved".

This plaque, half of which has been restored, was a boundary marker demonstrating the King's intention to put a stop to the indiscriminate expansion of Paris, because of the city's problems concerning supplies, policing, and population increase. Within the city boundaries, landowners could build houses with the front walls overlooking existing streets, but under no circumstances could they build new roads. Only construction work currently under way on buildings in the faubourgs could be completed. Parisians, recalcitrant by nature, did not take much notice of these prohibitions.

The plaque in Rue de Charenton is one of the few plaques – 294 in all – to have survived until today. It was put up on December 27th, 1727, on the wall of the "last house in the street near the country", on the corner of Rue de Picpus and Rue de Lamblardie. In 1910, historian Lucien Lambeau discovered half of the plaque lying among some tiles on the floor of a room at the back of a hardware shop at 304-6 Rue de Charenton. The owner of the building agreed to the plaque being fixed on the façade – and charged hundred francs!

Another plaque similar to this one can be seen at 4 Rue de Laborde in the 8th arrondissement.

"Borne by the wine"

PARC DE BERCY
RUE PAUL-BELMONDO
Métro: Bercy

P arc de Bercy is one of the most successful green spaces recently created in Paris. However, many Parisians regret the disappearance of the Bercy warehouses, whose romantic atmosphere, with their wine and spirit stores and the wine barrels, was reminiscent of Paris in bygone days, a subject dear to the heart of French photographer Robert Doisneau, who succeeded in capturing human emotions – love, sadness, happiness – experienced in everyday life in Paris and the suburbs. Under the shade of trees, one hundred years old, where thousands of birds have nested, the paved streets, criss-crossed by railway tracks and lined with old warehouses, used to be a source of delight: the smell of damp wood and corks, and the bouquet of a glass of wine sneaked from a broken old vat at the wine merchant's.

Although difficult to imagine today, this place used to bustle with activity, as barges full of barrels unloaded their cargo onto the quays. The wine merchants used to take their clients to the Golden Apple Inn, where, after a meal washed down with plenty of wine, "juicy" contracts were signed.

In 1979, bulldozers put an end to more than one and a half centuries of wine trading, destroying many renowned wine stores such as "Joninon et Saillard" and "Badoc". The Sports Centre with its lawns defying the laws of gravitation was built on the site, followed a few years later by the Treasury.

Parc de Bercy – a garden commemorating the past – has kept the old, paved warehouse roads. Preserved old buildings, some of them in ruins, and themed areas, beneath the centenarian trees, help recall Bercy's shattered past. A herb garden enables children to become familiar with the different scents of herbs, and to discover vines and fruit trees trained on espaliers. Despite all this, is Bercy really like it used to be, since, by force of circumstance, it is becoming more difficult to leave, "borne by the wine towards a celestial, enchanting sky", in the exalting words of poet Charles Baudelaire?

The colours and the atmosphere of the old Bercy area
are a source of inspiration to photographers and writers.

Russia overlooking Alsace

"LITTLE RUSSIA" AND "LITTLE ALSACE"
22 RUE BARRAULT/10 AND 7 RUE DAVIEL
Métro: Glacière or Corvisart

At the end of a passage through an ordinary-looking building at 22 Rue Barrault, behind a glass door, and at the top of some rather steep, cement steps to a terrace level with the third floor of the building overlooking the street, an unusually charming sight awaits you – rows of attractive terraced houses, decorated with flower pots, just the place for sleepy cats. Known as "Little Russia",

this group of houses was built originally for the employees – most of them Russian – of a taxi company, whose vehicles were kept in the garage below. This terrace overlooks Cité Daviel, nicknamed "Little Alsace", located at 10 Rue Daviel, a right turning off Rue Barrault. The wide entrance opens into a rectangular courtyard lined with gabled, brick houses, designed by

Left: Little Russia.
Below: Little Alsace.

architect Jean Walter in 1912 for a company called "Habitation familiale". There are a total of forty houses which can accommodate up to 302 people. The architect was awarded a silver medal by the Seine Regional Council Sponsor Committee. These attractive houses, unfortunately not very well looked after, are built around an area of 550 square metres, and have been on the list of picturesque, City of Paris sites since 1979. Just as pretty as Cité Daviel is Villa Daviel, a cul-de-sac located at no. 7 on the opposite side of the street, with its unpretentious yellow and red brick houses and their small gardens, where the fuchsia, roses and wisteria reflect the owners' taste in flowers. Two very special places which we hope we can go on visiting for a long time to come.

107

A venue for artists

CITÉ FLEURIE
65 BOULEVARD ARAGO
Métro: Glacière or Saint-Jacques

Domela who used to live in Cité Fleurie, gives access to this private residence. Two long wooden buildings line both sides of a passage. The buildings are divided into 29 workshop-cum-apartments still occupied by artists. An 18th-century residence, whose main entrance is in Rue Léon-Maurice-Nordmann, backs onto a garden at the far end.

In 1880, Cité Fleurie was constructed on a piece of wasteland with building material recuperated from the site of the 1878 World Fair. Many famous people have been through its doors. Paul Gauguin lived at Daniel de Monfreid's home for a time; Modigliani was put up by Mexican painter Angel Zanaga at no. 9; Art-Nouveau painter Eugène Grasset (creator of Larousse publishing house's emblem), painter Jean-Paul Laurens, and sculptors Jean Boucher and César Domela, all worked there. In 1934, an anti-nazi library, where it was possible to read all the "subversive" literature being burned in Germany, was founded at no. 18, later to be pillaged by the Germans during the Occupation.

In 1971, this oasis of greenery nearly disappeared. However, after a long, hard battle, the residence was preserved and listed.

Opposite a grey, oblong building on a dreary part of Boulevard Arago, Cité Fleurie is a secluded haven of greenery, which had a narrow escape from the bulldozers, and is something of a miracle. A long metal gate next to the little Arago public garden, where there is a sculpture by the late César

The Bièvre poplar trees

SQUARE RENÉ-LE-GALL
43 RUE CORVISART
Métro: Corvisart

River Bièvre, whose name is derived from the latin word, *biver* (beaver), still runs through Paris – in the form of a sewer! When it was covered over at the beginning of the century, it was nothing more than a repulsive, muddy stream, whose foul water washed along the evil-smelling waste from the numerous tanneries on its banks.

Not far from Rue Croulebarbe, the river divided into two arms which joined up again a little further on, thus forming a tree-planted island. A century ago, it had small gardens which the Gobelins' tapestry factory put at the disposal of its employees.

Square René-Le-Gall was opened to the public in 1938, and its oldest section covers most of the island. Old poplar trees, some of which have been replaced with hornbeams, still follow the river's former course.

Architect Jean-Charles Moreux took into account the layout of the island's former paths when he designed this country-style garden, prettily decorated with an obelisk, flower-decked arbours, and rocks.

Below Rue Berbier-du-Mets, a chestnut tree, more than a hundred years old, towers over younger specimens from other countries: chestnut trees from the Balkans, locust trees from North America, sophoras from Japan, walnut trees from the Caucasus, pine trees from the Himalays, etc.

A beautiful parade of trees indicating the former course of River Bièvre.

Juice of the vine

36 RUE NATIONALE
Métro: Nationale

There is a surprise in store for you at 36 Rue Nationale in the form of several tiny allotments similar to those that used to be cultivated on the fortifications until the thirties. Even today, allotments can be found in some suburban towns such as Saint-Denis, Bagnolet, Stains or Villeneuve-Saint-Georges.

Brightly painted, tumbledown, wooden sheds and a few carefully tended vines... The festive atmosphere of the grape harvest makes September the best time to pay a visit. The timeless quality of the place, amidst a concrete forest of high-rise buildings, ought to be preserved at all costs.

Another spot worth visiting is a small cul-de-sac (Impasse Nationale) not far from here at no. 54, and, before leaving this area, a walk down Passage Bourgoin, with its charming little houses cherished by their fortunate owners, is strongly recommended.

A leafy paradise

CITÉ VERTE
147 RUE LÉON-MAURICE-NORDMANN
Métro: Glacière

property developer's convincing arguments, the religious community who owned the premises, was prepared to sell them without regret. After protests from various sources, several building permits were refused, and the site was listed on August 6th, 1979. Since then, life has gone on quietly.

About twenty artists' ateliers line a paved path. Abandoned works of art stand amidst ivy trailing everywhere: an "Egyptian" bas-relief, and, further on, another bas-relief of a pack of cyclists in action, along with a mutilated statue serving as a flowerpot holder. Except perhaps for the noble-looking, white, overgrown façade, ornamented with pilasters, near the entrance, the buildings themselves are not very interesting – as is often the case with housing developments of this nature – but they are, nevertheless, very attractive! Though it is sheltered from the bustle of city life, Cité Verte is very much a part of Paris.

Cité Verte – overgrown with vegetation of all kinds – looks like a survivor of rampant city planning. In 1977, moved by a

The "White Queen's" castle

17 AND 19 RUE DES GOBELINS
Métro: Gobelins

Near Boulevard Arago, the tiny street called Rue des Gobelins, formerly Rue de Bièvre, seems to have escaped the attention of city planners, judging by its general state of disrepair. At no. 17, at the far end of a factory courtyard surrounded by unsightly brick workshops, stands an ancient, gabled residence: the legendary White Queen's castle. Books about Paris, written in the 19th century, never fail to mention this strange building, giving detailed, colourful – though invariably untrue – accounts of the house's history. Today, everyone knows that no White Queen – not even Blanche de Navarre, Blanche de Castille or Blanche de Bourgogne – ever set foot in the house at 17 Rue des Gobelins.

It was not so much a private house as a dyeing workshop, built by the Gobelin family in the 16th century. Its current state of neglect means that the outside of the house can be visited free of charge. When the building was listed, the elegant, timbered gallery, adjoining the cart archway leading into a weed-infested courtyard, was completely restored. By comparison, the big, three-storeyed building is in very bad condition, and deserves better treatment. However, it is the subject of a legal battle between the City of Paris and its owners.

Joris-Karl Huysmans described the building – a tannery at the time – in very vivid terms when he visited it in 1900: "It comprises vast, beamed rooms and spacious workshops where leather is cut and curried, for this little castle is, in fact, a tannery. Down below, along the length of an enormous room, whose slippery paved floor stretches out like a quagmire smelling of latrines and hot vinegar, stands a gigantic tank, parallel to the River Bièvre. And in the courtyard, it looks as if colossal cauldrons, dug into the ground, are boiling away; these are the tuns and vats where the skins lie soaking."

Next door, at no. 19, there is another house dating from the same period and which was used for a similar purpose. Both houses used to overlook the River Bièvre which is covered today by Rue Berbier-du-Mets.

Legend has it that this building, in a deplorable state, is the castle of the White Queen. However, not a single royal queen has ever set foot in the house, and history cannot tell us where the name comes from.

A breath of fresh air!

PITIÉ-SALPÊTRIÈRE HOSPITAL
47 BOULEVARD DE L'HÔPITAL
Métro: Saint-Marcel

A former explosives' factory, Salpêtrière became a hospital in the 17th century. Louis XIV's intention was to cram in all the vagabonds and beggars of Paris. In 1684, it became a women's prison.

Go through the main entrance, turn left and walk down the arched passage (Division Mazarin), and then down another passage leading to Division Montyon. Once through the porchway, you will see on your left the former prison buildings where prostitutes and common law criminals were locked up. Rue Saint-Félix, an 18th-century alley, runs alongside the prison, and a low building on the other side served as lodgings for the archers who rounded up the prostitutes. As Rue Saint-Félix bends to the right, you will see the former explosives' factory straight ahead, a magnificent restored building. If you go round it on the right-hand side, you will find some steps leading up to three one-storeyed buildings, the remains of the mentally handicapped women's quarters created in 1789. Each of the 600 inmates was locked up in a very small cell, a few metres square. Semicircular benches can still be seen securely fixed to the outside wall of the middle building. The guards used to chain the women to them so that the latter might benefit from the fresh air, a theory dear to the hearts of late 18th-century hygiene experts.

An orangery for Watteau

3 BIS RUE DES GOBELINS
Métro: Gobelins

At the far end of this courtyard, you will find a very old, two-storeyed building on the right-hand side. Sometimes wrongly called Hôtel Mascarini, it first belonged to a very famous family in district, the Gobelins. Then, in 1686, the manor house was bought by wealthy dyer Jean Gluck, who made some radical alterations. His nephew and heir, Jean de Jullienne, took up residence there, and added to the magnificence of the house with his collection of carefully selected paintings, rare pieces of furniture and bronze statues.

Despite the ravages of time, the building is still fine sight. If you go up the front steps, at the top of which there is an attractive *mascaron*, you can see the house's straight staircase, originally fitted with a beautiful, wooden balustrade.

A stroll down the passage on the right will lead you to the wing built at right angles – remains of an orangery facing north, laid out by Jean de Jullienne, a great art collector and patron of rococo painter Watteau. The former used to hold lavish painting exhibitions in this orangery, almost twenty metres long, supported by tall Tuscan columns, and very tastefully restored by its current occupiers.

Streets where cats may meditate

CITÉ FLORALE (OR FLORÉALE)
36-8 AND 50-4 RUE BRILLAT-SAVARIN
RER: Cité Universitaire

the big city-planning developments of the sixties and seventies, some delightful spots did manage to survive.

One of these is Cité Florale – next to Place de Rungis, a stone's throw from Boulevards Jourdan and Kellermann – built towards the end of the twenties. Its site, a pond that had been filled in during the 19th century, could not support the weight of tall buildings. Consequently, detached houses in all sorts of architectural styles were built, and they make a very pretty sight for anyone who cares to stroll down here.

Wisteria, morning glory, orchids, and mimosa are the names of these tranquil, barely congested streets. Hush, lest we disturb the cats meditating in the sun!

Although the 13th arrondissement did not, for the most part, escape the onslaught of excavators, particularly active during

Meadows, mills and poplars

SQUARE DES PEUPLIERS AND RUE DIEULAFOY
74 RUE DU MOULIN-DES-PRÉS
Métro: Tolbiac

The gabled houses in Rue Dieulafoy.

In the 18th century, fields and arable land stretched out along the River Bièvre, and a path lined with poplar trees crossed the plain. The trees have long since disappeared, but the names on blue and green plaques on every street corner bear witness to them. Near the crossroads at Rue du Moulin-des-Prés, whose name – Windmill-in-the-Fields – speaks for itself, there is a curious, triangular-shaped cul-de-sac called Square des Peupliers (poplars). To anyone enjoying a quiet walk round this tiny square, with its little houses nestling behind their railings, the hustle and bustle of city life seems a long way off. It was built in 1926, as was most of the district between Rue Ernest-et-Henri-Rousselle and Place de l'Abbé-Georges-Hénocque. This area used to be wasteland with just a few ragmen's sheds dotted here and there.

Rue Dieulafoy is easily reached via Place de l'Abbé-Georges-Hénocque. The houses with their attractive, pointed roofs all look alike, and are similar to those in Rue Santos-Dumont in the 15th arrondissement.

A mere shadow
of the Cordelières Convent

INSIDE BROCA HOSPITAL ENCLOSURE, CORNER OF RUES PASCAL AND JULLIENNE
Métro: Gobelins

Some ruins – the remains of the Cordelières Convent – next to Broca Hospital, are a rather unexpected sight. The nuns of the order of Saint Clare, François d'Assise's sister, came here in 1289; the buildings were extended and improved by Marguerite de Provence, widow of Louis IX, known as Saint Louis, who led the Sixth Crusade. The nuns lived for years in this peaceful convent in Saint Marcel, a village in the country. During the French Revolution, the abbey was parcelled out, and the church and two sides of the cloisters were destroyed. In 1836, the former convent was converted into a hospital.

In 1974, the tall structures with traces of ribbed vaults and medieval buttresses had become old and dilapidated, and were replaced by today's modern buildings. In the wards inside, rows of columns with capitals represented more tangible evidence of a bygone age. Even some of the original framework, a masterpiece by journeymen, had survived.

There are still some remains in the hospital garden – former dormitory windows, shafts of columns and capitals dating back to the 13th and 14th centuries. These ancient stones are a final reminder of the existence of the Cordelières Convent.

Workshops in the cloister

THE FORMER CONVENT OF THE ENGLISH NUNS
28 RUE DES TANNERIES
Métro: Glacière

There are some modest workshops under the arches of a 17th-century cloister at the far end of a beautiful, paved courtyard. The cloister used to be part of the English Nuns' Convent, named after the English Benedictine nuns who took refuge here in 1664 when fleeing persecution of the Catholics. The first Mother Superior was no other than Sister Brigitte More, granddaughter of Sir Thomas More, former Lord Chancellor of England.

The courtyard was converted into a cloister in 1693, and the chapel, which used to stand on the present site of the concierge's office, was restored in 1784. After a first escape from persecution of the Catholics in England, the English nuns, along with their French counterparts, suffered further persecution during the French Revolution. Sequestered in their convent, stripped of their belongings, they were finally deported back to their own country in 1794. England – rarely daunted by paradoxical situations – welcomed back with open arms its fellow citizens who had suffered at the hands of its barbaric neighbours on the Continent!

The lovely Adrienne

VILLA ADRIENNE AND LA ROCHEFOUCAULD HOSPICE
15 AND 19 AVENUE DU GÉNÉRAL-LECLERC
Métro: Denfert-Rochereau

Villa Adrienne, built around a large, rectangular garden, is a veritable square affording strollers a quiet rest from their travels. This group of late 19th-century buildings is made of brick and stone, and each entrance bears the name of a famous person: Watteau, Berlioz, Pascal, Lavoisier, etc. A small door – Delacroix – opens into a tiny garden. Down one side of the square, hidden behind the foliage, private houses have taken precedence over public housing. When you leave Villa Adrienne, turn left and go to the La Rochefoucauld old people's home at no. 15. As soon as you enter, you will appreciate the straight lines of this beautiful building, formerly the Royal Nursing Home, founded in 1780 near the former Enfer tollgate. It took in soldiers and clergymen who had fallen on hard times. Living conditions cannot have been exactly cramped at first, since there were only twenty-three inmates when the French Revolution started!

There is a good view of the house's rear wall from Avenue René-Coty. Just in front of the wall, there is a small, curious-looking structure – an inspection chamber – originally connected to the Arcueil aqueduct, and which controlled the water mains supplying water to the nursing home (see also pp. 122-23).

Meridian marker

PARC MONTSOURIS
BOULEVARD JOURDAN ENTRANCE
RER: Cité Universitaire

Parc Montsouris, a charming landscape garden, and the nearby Cité Universitaire are the lungs of south Paris. The park was designed by expert landscape gardener and engineer Alphand, who worked closely with Baron Haussmann, city planner under Napoleon III.

Near the exit on Boulevard Jourdan stands a curious-looking stone stela with a round hole though the top. Dated 1806, it bears the inscription: "Du règne de..." (in the reign of). Napoleon I's name has been removed, probably during the French Restoration (1814-30).

The stone marker indicates the Paris meridian, for a long time the prime meridian used by sailors until it was supplanted by the Greenwich meridian in 1884. The Paris meridian links up Dunkerque with Perpignan on the map of France. In the north of Paris, another marker, older than its southern counterpart, is unfortunately under lock and key on private property near Moulin de la Galette in Montmartre.

In 1806, while still a student at École Polytechnique (French engineering school), François Arago was given the task of prolonging the meridian as far as the Balearic Islands. As a tribute to him, France asked Dutch sculptor Jan Dibbets to create a "virtual" monument: 135 medallions in copper, zinc and tin, embedded in the ground all along the Paris meridian. The first of these medallions can be seen a few metres away from the stone marker.

The King's turncock

THE TURNCOCK'S HOUSE
42 AVENUE DE L'OBSERVATOIRE
For visits, phone 01.48.87.74.31. (2-6 pm). Métro: Denfert-Rochereau or RER: Port-Royal

Thanks to the perseverance of volunteers belonging to the Association for the preservation and enhancement of historical Paris, the basement of the oldest house in the 14th arrondissement has been preserved and restored. This small, light-coloured stone structure with its flat-tiled roof played a major role in the history of water in Paris, and was listed in 1994.

Between 1613 and 1623, Queen Marie de Médicis had the famous Arcueil aqueduct built, in order to supply her Luxembourg Palace gardens with water. This superb structure was erected on the site of a similar construction dating back to the Gallo-Roman era.

Between 1619 and 1623, the "Main Inspection Chamber of the Observatory", or more simply the "turncock's house", built on the aqueduct, which diverted water from Rungis, was surrounded by fields, a few farms and two windmills. Thomas Francini, General Manager of the King's water supply and fountains, worked and lived here with his family. His descendents occupied the premises until 1784. This small building comprises a ground floor, a first floor and a converted loft.

The basement is divided into three rooms equipped with decanting reservoirs, one for the King, one for the town, and one for the Carmelites. Water from the aqueduct poured into each of the reservoirs, and was then carried by three lead pipes of different diameters to the Luxembourg gardens, the religious communities of the area, and several fountains in Paris. In the presence of the city aldermen, these water mains were inaugurated on May 19th, 1623; they continued to supply water to the Medicis fountain in Luxembourg Gardens until 1904.

Today, water from the aqueduct no longer passes through the turncock's house. An enormous control reservoir with a capacity of 1,030 cubic metres, designed to reprocess water at night, was closed down in 1874 when the Montsouris reservoir came on line.

Left: The control reservoir. Above: Starting point of the three pipes "du Roi", "des Carmélites" and "de la Ville" ("King", "Carmelites" and "the City").

Quiet times in Alésia

VILLA D'ALÉSIA
111 RUE D'ALÉSIA/39 BIS RUE DES PLANTES
Métro: Alésia

Built in 1897, Villa d'Alésia, formerly called Villa Parquet, is a tiny right-angled street linking Rue d'Alésia with Rue des Plantes. Its greenery and its small buildings, some of which are surrounded by vast gardens, make a pleasant change from the noise of the traffic nearby.

Large workshops are still to be found here, a reminder that craft industries continue to operate, albeit less actively, in the 14th arrondissement. In fact, around 1910, there used to be a printing works, where only deaf-mutes were employed. Now, there is very little industrial activity here, except for handicrafts: a potter, on request, will create all sorts of shapes imaginable. The peace and quiet of a street in the country, just a stone's throw from the heart of the capital.

Country streets in Paris

SQUARE DE MONTSOURIS (AND NEIGHBOURING STREETS)
ALONGSIDE PARC MONTSOURIS
RER: Cité Universitaire

All along Rue Nansouty and Rue Émile-Deutsch-de-la-Meurthe, bordering Parc Montsouris, there are some delightful little alleys, a veritable paradise on the fringes of the 14th arrondissement, best visited in spring when the lilac is in bloom.

The first of these side streets, as you come from Avenue René-Coty, is Square de Montsouris. The house at the far end was designed by Le Corbusier. As you come into Avenue Reille, notice the elegant, glass-fronted buildings of the Montsouris reservoir. In order to reach the next street, go back down Square de Montsouris. Rue Georges-Braque is a cul-de-sac built in 1927, called Rue du Douanier until 1976, when it was named after painter Georges Braque. He lived at no. 6 in a brick and concrete house-cum-atelier designed by architect Auguste Perret. The atelier on the second floor has a very big window.

Continue up Rue Nansouty towards Boulevard Jourdan and stroll down the other alleys and cul-de-sacs bordering the park: Rue du Parc-de-Montsouris, Villa du Parc-Montsouris (a real headache for those delivering mail!), Impasse Nansouty. Each one is appealing in its own way, demonstrating, not for the first time, how Paris can sometimes resemble a sleepy country town.

Above: Villa Hallé.
Opposite: The semicircular row of houses in Rue Hallé.

Orléans village

RUE AND VILLA HALLÉ
36 RUE HALLÉ
Métro: Mouton-Duvernet

The architectural styles of the buildings erected along a curve in Rue Hallé, not far from Avenue du Général-Leclerc, are amazingly different. Rue Hallé – along with Rue Ducouédic and Rue Rémy-Dumoncel – was part of a housing development, known as the "Village d'Orléans", built around 1830 on parcels of land, which had been put up for sale for this purpose. The original plan was to build houses in similar styles, but this was never to be! However, the results of the city-planning operation along Rue Hallé add to the charm of this quiet neighbourhood. Villa Hallé – a small, curved cul-de-sac – starts at no. 36, behind the remains of a gate topped with spikes.

There is something about this cul-de-sac which is reminiscent of villages on the outskirts of Paris with their small houses in contrasting styles and their tiny back gardens. It was undoubtedly because of the atmosphere here that one of the houses was used as the home of the heroine – played by Catherine Deneuve – of Francis Girod's film, *Le Bon Plaisir*.

The windmill of Charity

MONTPARNASSE CEMETERY
3 BOULEVARD EDGAR-QUINET
Métro: Edgar-Quinet or Montparnasse-Bienvenüe

Clearly visible from the streets around Montparnasse cemetery, a tower-like structure looking rather lonely and out of place in the middle of this graveyards, is no other than the remains of "Moulin de la Charité", used today to store gravediggers' equipment. This windmill is the last of many that used to exist around Mont Parnasse in the 18th century.

Strictly speaking, it is probably a 14th- or 15th-century smock mill whose roof – originally mobile and fitted with vanes – used to rotate on a revolving shaft.

As was often the case in those days, the windmill served both as a tavern and a flour mill. The miller would serve some *galette* (a round, flat cake) and a small glass of wine. Many students from Clermont College (now Louis-le-Grand High School) used to go to Moulin de la Charité. As they were pro-Jesuits, they steered clear of Moulin des Trois-Cornets nearby, a favourite haunt of Jansenists.

It is difficult to imagine today that there used to be lots of windmills like this one – complete with vanes – all around Montparnasse station.

The artists' residence

VILLA SEURAT
101 RUE DE LA TOMBE-ISSOIRE
Métro: Alésia

Villa Seurat – a charming cul-de-sac – was created at the instigation of architect André Lurçat who spotted some land in 1919, and persuaded its owner to divide it up into lots. A solution had to be found to the serious housing crisis facing the "Montparnos" (artists and writers working and living in the Montparnasse district between the two World Wars), who had to leave their base and move to this district, not far from the city fortifications. The place was to become a veritable laboratory for experiments in architecture.

The first order came from Jean Lurçat, the architect's brother, renowned for his revival of the art of tapestry. In July 1924, André Lurçat built him an L-shaped house with a square courtyard at no. 4. This order was followed by others from painters Marcel Gromaire and Édouard Goerg; the striking feature of both these ateliers at nos. 3 and 3 bis is their slightly rounded façades, somewhat reminiscent of Villa Laroche in the 16th arrondissement (see p. 145).

André Lurçat continued to receive orders from painters, sculptors, and writers (nos. 1, 5, 8, 9, 11), and famous architect Auguste Perret designed a building (no. 7) for sculptress Chana Orloff.

Part of the cul-de-sac's attraction is that the avant-garde façades of the ateliers and houses are singularly alike. It can also pride itself on having been home to Expressionist painter Soutine and, at no. 18, writer Henry Miller, who wrote his famous books, *Tropic of Cancer* and *Tropic of Capricorn*, while he was here.

Three very dissimilar houses

3 BIS, 5 AND 7 RUE CASSINI
Métro: Saint-Jacques or RER: Port-Royal

R ue Cassini can pride itself on having been the home of some very important people, beginning with the famous family of astronomers – four generations – who lived here and gave the street its name.

From 1828 to 1835, writer Honoré de Balzac lived in a house which used to be no. 1. This was where he started planning his masterpiece, *La Comédie Humaine* (The Human Comedy), and he had his first work published while he was still living there. At the end of his garden, a small door communicated with the Observatory gardens, enabling the writer to converse with the pupils of that establishment. Astronomist, physicist and politician François Arago, his neighbour, liked to reminisce about that time: "... from this window on the terrace, I could see his candles flickering: we both used to work late into the night, my eyes were riveted on the sky, his head was bent over a sheet of paper. And perhaps the astronomer was not the one who saw the furthest!"

The exact site of Balzac's house, no longer standing, has never been known with any certainty; it probably stood on the south side of Rue Cassini.

On the other hand, three beautiful, big houses, built between 1903 and 1906, are well and truly visible.

Bricks have been used to fill in the reinforced concrete structure of the house at no. 3, undoubtedly the most refined and the most elegant of the three houses. It was built for painter Lucien Simon who was responsible for some of the ceilings of the Senate.

The house at no. 5 is an austere, brick, medieval-looking building, erected for painter Jean-Paul Laurens, whose paintings still ornament one of the City Hall's reception rooms.

The building at no. 7 is in a freely-inspired, neoclassical style, and was designed for painter Czernikowski.

Three different styles, all created by one man, painter and architect Louis Süe, who was not averse to a certain degree of eclecticism. He was also responsible for the artists' ateliers at 126 Boulevard du Montparnasse (see p. 132).

Rendezvous in hell

PASSAGE D'ENFER
RUE CAMPAGNE-PREMIÈRE/249 BOULEVARD RASPAIL
Métro: Raspail or Edgar-Quinet

Passage d'Enfer, an L-shaped, private road, owes its name to the area around Boulevard d'Enfer (Hell), renamed Boulevard Raspail in 1887.

The rear façade at nos. 24-7 is that of a superb building at nos. 31-4 Rue Campagne-Première, decorated with ceramics and well worth a visit (architect André Arfvidson, 1911). There is a faded façade of a former dry cleaner's, and the other buildings, all alike, are being cleaned. The cul-de-sac, which runs into Boulevard Raspail, is a haven of peace amid the hustle and bustle of Montparnasse.

The privacy of your own home

126 BOULEVARD DU MONTPARNASSE
Métro: Vavin

A fine, freestone façade decorated with a string course of floral motifs has two entrances, the right-hand one leading to a staircase, and the left-hand, to a courtyard. There is a majestic, luxurious air about this extraordinary complex, comprising apartments and ateliers. They are privately-owned and rented apartment blocks, designed by architect Louis Süe, and built in concrete covered with mortar. The six- and eight-storeyed apartment blocks were first rented to young couples who were artists, and sleeping partner Mr Moreau had one of the privately-owned blocks. Privacy is an important feature. The windows are tiered, letting in a maximum amount of light, while hiding the big gardens at the back. French socialist statesman Léon Blum once lived on the first floor of the building overlooking the street.

A "mobile" manor house

HÔTEL DE MASSA
38 RUE DU FAUBOURG-SAINT-JACQUES
Visit to gardens: phone 01.43.07.09.69. Métro: Saint-Jacques or RER: Port-Royal

Hôtel de Massa, a strictly private establishment, stands in a shady garden next to the Observatory park, and is the home of the "Société des Gens de Lettres" (Literary Society). The most unusual feature concerning this beautiful manor house is that it used to stand elsewhere – on the corner of Rue La Boétie and the Champs-Elysées – before being moved to this quiet spot in the 14th arrondissement in 1927.

It was built in 1784 in the middle of a large park, and was the scene of lavish parties, elegant receptions and romantic encounters. Seized as national property during the French Revolution, the manor house was later allotted to the Italian ambassador who invited Napoleon and Josephine to the brilliant receptions he gave there.

Many years later, in 1926, when the Champs-Elysées became more popular again, two property developers – Théophile Bader, director of department store Galeries Lafayette, and André Lévy – bought the manor house and its parkland with the intention of building a vast complex on its site. Unfortunately for them, the edifice was listed. In order to get round this difficulty, they offered to finance the dismantling and reassembling of the house elsewhere, which they did. The harmonious dimensions of Hôtel de Massa were noted on a plan, each stone numbered, and the pieces carried across Paris to the present site. The job took two years to complete, and required sixty workers possessing a variety of skills.

In April 1929, the Literary Society held its first session at Hôtel de Massa, on the very site where a resident from Rue Cassini nearby (see p. 130) used to stroll a century earlier: his name was Honoré de Balzac... the first president of the "Société des Gens de Lettres".

Port-Libre Prison

PORT-ROYAL CLOISTER (BAUDELOCQUE HOSPITAL)
123-25 BOULEVARD DE PORT-ROYAL/2-22 RUE DU FAUBOURG-SAINT-JACQUES
Chapel open on Sunday mornings at 10.30 am. (Mass). RER: Port-Royal

Most of Paris' cloisters have disappeared, and many people are unaware of the existence of those that have survived. Such is the case of the Port-Royal Convent cloister on Boulevard Port-Royal.

In 1204, Mathieu de Montmorency and his wife, Mathilde de Garlande, founded Port-Royal-des-Champs Abbey in the Chevreuse valley. In 1603, Mother Angélique Arnauld bought the former Hôtel de Clagny – in Rue de la Bourbe near Rue Saint-Jacques – and the surrounding land. In 1626, the nuns of the order of the Blessed Sacrament, won over by Jansenist ideas, moved in. Mother Angélique had some more convent buildings put up.

Port-Royal-de-Paris became a leading centre for religious thinking, and served as a retreat for scholars such as Lemaître de Sacy, Nicole, Abbot de Saint-Cyran, and sometimes Blaise Pascal, French philosopher, mathematician and physicist.

The convent's history is marked by persecution, and the eventual disappearance of the Jansenists; during the French Revolution it was closed down, and, in 1793, converted into a prison – known as the "Port-Libre Prison". The prisoners set up a phalanstery, whereby the rich financed the poor, and an internal organization to ensure that prison management was under their control. However, many of its inmates – politician Malesherbes and chemist Lavoisier among others – ended up on the scaffold during the Reign of Terror. In 1795, the Convention decided to use the convent for accommodating foundlings and their wet nurses along with women about to give birth.

Arrows indicating "chapelle" at the entrance will lead you to the ancient buildings. The cloister is three-sided, and, on the north side, there is a small door opening into the chapel, whose nave has just one row of benches. The chapel was designed by architect Lepautre (1646-48), and used to be decorated with Philippe de Champaigne's extraordinary paintings, now hanging in provincial museums as well as in the Louvre. The metal screen separating the chancel from the nave serves as a reminder of the austere lives the nuns led here.

Master glassworker
in a secluded square

SQUARE VERGENNES, 279 RUE DE VAUGIRARD
Métro: Vaugirard

Master glassworker Barillet's house stands at the far end of Square Vergennes, a quiet, attractive cul-de-sac. Mallet-Stevens designed the building in 1932 for Barillet, whom he regarded as his friend and colleague, and who often accepted orders from the architect, and supplied him with glass on many occasions.

Mallet-Stevens put the living quarters on the fourth floor and the workshops for cutting glass and creating mosaics on the three floors below, and placed the entire weight of the building on a single, central, loadbearing post – an astonishing feat of engineering. The features of the façade make it possible to distinguish the workshops on the left – behind big glass windows – from the offices on the right – in the narrow, rounded part of the building. Today's glass windows are not those designed by Mallet-Stevens; his windows were composed of small rectangles, made wider at the top in order to amplify the perspective of the building. An awning over the front entrance is surmounted by a narrow, stained-glass window by Barillet, extending up to the top of the building.

Château Violet

SQUARE VIOLET
PLACE VIOLET
Métro: Félix-Faure

Château Violet, partly visible from Square Violet.

There are some very old trees in Square Violet, a garden not far from Rue du Commerce, and in particular a cottonwood tree, twenty-five metres high.

Château Violet, the rather tall building in the enclosure of the neighbouring fire station, partly concealed by the wall in the garden, used to be the residence of speculator Léonard Violet, who created the district. The Square itself was built on his property.

In 1824, Léonard Violet, along with Alphonse Letellier, bought some vast pieces of land which were part of the Grenelle agricultural plains.

Instead of using it as arable land, he built a new town called "Beaugrenelle", complete with shops, a place of worship, a theatre, a river port, and an industrial site. The streets were planned from scratch, and right-angled intersections were created, still a rare sight on this scale in Paris today. The building work was completed very rapidly; it took only a few years to transform the rural area into a town.

The house, still called "Château de Grenelle", which first belonged to Léonard Violet, had to be sold, as the latter suffered a reversal of fortune around 1927. He was compelled to live in small house in the street named after him. However, he continued to follow up the development of what was to become a town in its own right, and was even a member of the town council for 36 years.

The "château" changed hands several times before being made into a fire station in 1860, and that is still its function today.

A tree in a church

SAINT-SÉRAPHIN-DE-SARROW CHURCH
91 RUE LECOURBE
Métro: Volontaires

Streets like Rue Lecourbe are hard to find these days. Its many, varied stalls take us back to the happy times when markets were lively and cheerful, with crowds of light-hearted Parisians jostling one another on their way to buy bread, poultry, and vegetables on Sundays. Some of the vendors call out to the customers, recommending the "extra fresh" peas or the "extraordinary" cherries. This busy shopping street is one of the oldest roads in the capital, and villages Meudon and Sèvres, just south of Paris, could be reached by it.

Such hustle and bustle in the street makes it difficult to imagine that behind one of its doors there is an incredibly peaceful place, with a timeless quality about it. The entrance of the nondescript, 19th-century building at no. 91 gives access to a passage leading to two small courtyards lined with attractive houses built in the same century. At the far end of the second one, there is a wooden chalet, housing Saint-Séraphin Church, topped with a sky-blue, onion-shaped dome. In 1933, the building – erected around a tree – was even smaller; today's church dates from 1974. The bottom part of the tree was preserved, and is still on view in this orthodox chapel, whose congregation is composed of members of the Russian community – descendants of "White Russian" immigrants – living in the 15th arrondissement. Many of them took up residence here, as well as in the 16th arrondissement, because of the proximity of the Citroën and Renault factories.

For a long time, the "White Russians" in this district had their own shops, restaurants, pharmacies, and school. Parties and receptions – the most well-known of these being the "Russian drivers' party" – enabled exiles to get together, thanks to the efforts of a large number of associations.

The shadow of the slaughterhouses

PARC GEORGES-BRASSENS
36 BIS RUE DES MORILLONS
Métro: Convention or Porte de Vanves

and eighty thousand pigs were killed there every year. Near Rue Castagnary, workers in the meat industry took over from the slaughterhouse workers, and prepared salami, paté, salted meats and cooked pork meats of all kinds.

Closed down in 1978, most of the buildings in Rue des Morillons – except for the two octroi buildings, the auction-room bell-tower, now overlooking a pool, and two horse-market buildings bordering Rue Brancion (site of a well-known, weekend, antiquarian and second-hand book market) – were demolished to make way for Georges-Brassens Park and Silvia-Monfort Theatre. Decorative items such as the portal, moved to the corner of Rue des Morillons, and the two proud-looking bronze bulls from the entrance, modelled by Auguste Cain, have also been preserved. A climbing wall for children has been made out of masses of overturned earth and stones from the old market halls, left over from the demolition.

There are vines at the top of the hill in the park along with a few buzzing beehives, and a "herb garden" near the entrance in Rue des Morillons, where you can take a pleasantly scented walk.

Vaugirard slaughterhouses were inaugurated in 1898, and, thereafter, life for the residents in the area was punctuated daily by a procession of pigs, horses and cattle going through the entrance in Rue des Morillons – one hundred and ten thousand cattle, seventy thousand calves, five hundred thousand sheep

A hive of activity

LA RUCHE
PASSAGE DE DANTZIG
Métro: Convention

There is a gigantic, rusty key at La Ruche's entrance; getting through the gate is easier for cats than it is for mere mortals.

La Ruche (beehive) – its name comes from the layout of ateliers around the central staircase, resembling cells in a beehive – was a wine pavilion at the 1900 World Fair. Erected by the team working for Gustave Eiffel, designer of the Eiffel Tower, the building was later auctioned, and bought by Boucher, a sculptor in vogue at the time, who wished to provide accommodation for artists less fortunate than himself. Once reassembled on some wasteland near Rue de Vaugirard, and fitted with the gates originating from the "Palais de la Femme" (a hostel for women in the 11th arrondissement), La Ruche was officially inaugurated in 1902.

Boucher, who affectionately referred to his protégés as bees, took in Fernand Léger as soon as 1905. Later, many artists from central Europe and elswhere came to "gather nectar" at La Ruche. Chagall, Soutine, Modigliani, Archipenko, Zadkine, poet Apollinaire and writer Blaise Cendrars, all came to work in this centre of the School of Paris.

In the 60s, La Ruche was saved from demolition, thanks to action taken by Chagall and other artists, and to the then Minister for Arts, André Malraux, and was subsequently listed. La Ruche is still a hive of activity, where numerous painters and sculptors continue to dedicate themselves to art.

The conspirators' meeting place

THE FORMER GOLDEN SUN INN
226 RUE DE VAUGIRARD
Métro: Volontaires

The houses of Vaugirard village have suffered a great deal since the early 20th century, and it is difficult to imagine Rue de Vaugirard as it was in the 18th century – a path lined with low, country-style houses, down which mail coaches used to race.

At no. 226, however, one of the houses, the former Auberge du Soleil d'Or (Golden Sun Inn), has survived. Until recently, the passage opening onto the street was decorated with a wooden, 18th-century sign carved in the shape of a splendid sun surrounded by a halo of a thousand rays. Alleged to have been stolen, it has been replaced by an unsightly trompe l'oeil which seems to emphasize even more the neglected state of these old houses. It would appear that the building has been saved from demolition, thanks

to the efforts of an association of residents. The right wing overlooking the courtyard was knocked down, but the left wing and the main building fronting onto the street – the only original parts – were preserved. Hopefully, the Golden Sun will now be restored to its former glory.

This is where supporters of communist revolutionary Gracchus Babeuf planned the famous Grenelle camp conspiracy to set up a "Republic of Equals" in 1796. As Republicans, they felt that the Directory was too soft with the Royalists and too severe with partisans of the Republic. Seven or eight Jacobins left the inn on September 9th to rally the soldiers of the 21st regiment, camped in the Grenelle plain. However, the plot was denounced and ended in fiasco. The police came to the Golden Sun Inn, and made many arrests. Some managed to escape via a small alley, formerly Rue Cadot and now called Cour du Soleil-d'Or, leading to Rue Blomet.

A month later, the Golden Sun conspirators were executed by a firing squad at Grenelle, and the humble inn joined the ranks of buildings whose foundations have been shaken by the course of history.

A lemon tree in a telephone booth

VILLA SANTOS-DUMONT
Métro: Convention

Villa Santos-Dumont is a hidden paradise, easily accessible to the well-informed. If you come from Rue de Vouillé, you will find Villa Santos-Dumont – a leafy cul-de-sac with vines growing through the paving stones – about halfway down Rue Santos-Dumont, also a very peaceful street.

Many famous people such as sculptor Ossip Zadkine at no. 3, painter Victor Brauner at no. 10 bis, mosaicist Gatti at no. 15, and, two numbers further down, writer Jeanne Champion, have lived here. However, for Parisians, the most well-known

resident was without doubt singer and composer Georges Brassens, renowned for his songs about friendship, love and death; he also set to music poems by Hugo and Villon. Before moving to the house with the pointed roof at no. 42, Brassens used to live in Impasse Florimont in the 14th arrondissement where kind-hearted Jeanne le Bonniec from Brittany had put him up since the dark days of World War II. On her death one sad day in 1968, Brassens decided to move to Villa Santos-Dumont, almost in exile, even though it was only a stone's throw from the 14th arrondissement.

The singer spent his time here working and entertaining his lifelong friends, René Fallet, André Vers, Pierre Maguelon, to mention but a few; he valued friendship very highly.

One day, while resting in Saint-Gély-du-Fesc, between Sète and Montpellier in southwestern France, Brassens fell in love with a lemon tree. He wanted to take a cutting of it back to "Santos-Dumont", and when somebody objected that the poor plant would not survive the climate in Paris, he said he would buy a telephone booth for it.

However, his death on October 29th, 1981 did not leave Brassens time to carry out his plan.

"Plums are in season"

BALZAC'S HOUSE
47 RUE RAYNOUARD AND RUE BERTON
Open every day except Mondays and public holidays from 10 am to 5.40 pm. Métro: Passy

The back door of Balzac's house opens into Rue Berton, which enabled him to elude his creditors.

R ue Berton, with its streetlamps and zigzags, still looks like a street in the country, similar to those in the village of Passy in the mid-19th century. It runs alongside the former property of Madame de Lamballe, now the Turkish embassy.

Opposite, a 1793 boundary stone against the wall of Balzac's house still marks the dividing line between the Passy and Auteuil domains.

In 1840, Honoré de Balzac, author of *Le Père Goriot* (Father Goriot), was up to his eyes in debt, and moved from Ville-d'Avray to Rue Basse. The house, fairly isolated and surrounded by leafy trees, had a back door in Rue Berton, which enabled Balzac to elude his creditors. He opened his door only to those who knew the passwords: "Plums are in season", or "I am bringing lace from Belgium".

In 1960, Balzac's house (entrance in Rue Raynouard) was opened as a museum, and the public can now visit the writer's study where he wrote several of the novels making up his masterpiece, *La Comédie Humaine* (The Human Comedy). The tiny garden adjoining the museum is a good place for reading the novels of this highly creative writer, described rather unkindly by a contemporary as a "fat boy, with sharp eyes, dressed in a white waistcoat, with the bearing of a herbalist, the face of a butcher, and the look of gilder".

Birdsong in the trees

HAMEAU BOILEAU
38 RUE BOILEAU
Métro: Chardon-Lagache

Hameau Boileau is a housing development built on part of the former property of Nicolas Despréaux, known as Boileau, poet and critic. As you go in, you will see a gilded medallion, which calls to memory the poet's house, later to be occupied by painter Hubert Robert.

Printer and lithographer Rose-Joseph Lemercier bought the land in 1838 and divided it into lots with the help of architect L. C. T. Charpentier. Financial speculation in Auteuil was a fairly risky business, but there was a regular omnibus service between Paris and this outlying countryside, and the talents of 19th-century property developers were not to be underestimated. They knew how to promote their product, particularly when it "combined the convenience of city life with the pleasure of living in the country".

Whether neoclassical or rustic in style, the houses all looked very luxurious. The gothic-style country house at 24 Avenue Despréaux is the most striking example of the original buildings. The architect, Jean-Charles Danjoy, who also restored cathedrals, designed a charming edifice whose outstanding feature – a turret – emphasizes the medieval appearance of this imitation half-timbered house.

Other buildings are more reminiscent of the countryside around Auteuil in the past, such as the one at no. 21, opposite a house whose style is typical of architecture in the thirties. Two roads meet to form a tiny square from which radiate leafy cul-de-sacs where birds can be heard singing in the foliage on bright, sunny days.

Proletarians
in the 16th arrondissement…

VILLA MULHOUSE, 86 RUE BOILEAU
Métro: Exelmans

Of all the "villages" in the 16th arrondissement, Villa Mulhouse – a humble, working-class version of Hameau Boileau nearby – is the one whose history is the most moving. It comprises Villas Dietz-Monin, Émile-Meyer, Cheysson, and Avenue Georges-Rissler, and adjoins Auteuil cemetery.

Villa Cheysson is a surprisingly narrow road. Since they were first built, some of the one-storeyed houses have had an extra storey added, or the basement converted. Each house has a tiny front garden, the walls are overgrown with ivy, and fragrant flowers scent the air.

In 1835, Jean Dollfus, a spinning mill owner in Mulhouse, had some small, modest houses built for his employees; fifty years later, there were more than a thousand such houses. This inspired Émile Cacheux – author of a work praising the merits of workers' housing developments "where hygiene and moral standards go hand in hand" – to create the Passy-Auteuil Society for workers' housing developments in 1882. It was responsible for the building of Villa Mulhouse with its 67 houses, which were both practical and inexpensive, and provided several generations of workers with a minimum of space and comfort.

Nowadays, it is difficult to imagine the Point-du-Jour district as a working class area. As for Villa Mulhouse, the residents there do not appear to be very representative of the working classes these days!

Villa Dietz-Monin.

A visit to the great architect

LE CORBUSIER FOUNDATION (VILLAS JEANNERET AND LAROCHE)
8 AND 10 SQUARE DU DOCTEUR-BLANCHE
Tel: 01.42.88.41.53. Métro: Jasmin

Between 1924 and 1925, Charles-Édouard Jeanneret, best known as Le Corbusier, built two houses (nos. 8 and 10) at the far end of Square du Docteur-Blanche, a turning off Rue du Docteur-Blanche (no. 55). The first one was for his brother, Albert Jeanneret, and the second for a Swiss banker from Basel, Raoul Laroche.

The Jeanneret house was a family house complete with music room. The structure of the Laroche house, on the other hand, is more complex since a gallery was required to house Laroche's extraordinary collection of works of art by Braque, Picasso, Léger, and many other artists. Since the plot of land was small, and windows could not overlook neighbouring properties, Le Corbusier built a large hall extending to the top of the house. A staircase leads up to the main room, the gallery, where there is a ramp giving access to the library.

From the outside, the two buildings look very different, and yet there is an underlying connection between the convex volumes of the Laroche house and the flat façade of the house next door. In 1968, the Le Corbusier Foundation moved into the two buildings. It looks after the architect's estate, and is devoted to

acquainting the general public with his work. To this end, the architect's files are kept here, a public library has been opened, and exhibitions are regularly organized in the Laroche house.

A glimpse of the interior of the art gallery in the Laroche house.

"Eccentric house"

CASTEL BÉRANGER
14 RUE LA FONTAINE
Métro: Michel-Ange-Auteuil

Before creating the most unusual métro entrances in the world, architect Hector Guimard designed Castel Béranger in Rue La Fontaine. His idea was as unconventional as it was successful, a combination of advanced technology and unbridled imagination.

When the house was built in 1897, Parisians were fascinated, amused or disgusted by its design. It brought the young, thirty-year-old architect to the notice of the general public, and became his hallmark. Although not much care was taken to preserve many of Guimard's works, his

building in Rue La Fontaine continues to bear witness to the architect's unique talent. Everything about its atypical façade, from its strange seahorses, clinging to the corners of the brick walls, to the caricature of the architect's face set in the wrought-iron balconies, is a source of astonishment. Straight lines appear to have been banished.

You can go into courtyard where you will see a fountain and the stained glass decorating small windows on all floors.

The fact that the City of Paris awarded a prize to Guimard in the first competition for the best façade in 1898 did not alter the local residents' disapproval of what they called the "Devil's House" (because of the grimaces on the faces dotted all over the façade), also nicknamed "Castel Dérangé" (Crazy Castle).

In 1897, painter Paul Signac moved into one of the ateliers on the sixth floor. He called the house, "Eccentric House", and thought it was badly designed. Nevertheless, it was practical, light, and had a telephone, an uncommon feature in those days. Guimard thought of everything. He found his way into every apartment, and the decorations – curtains and wall coverings, furniture, doorhandles, locks – all

Details of one of the walls of the well-named "Devil's House".

bore his hallmark. He was able to do this thanks to highly skilled artisans, experts in wrought iron, brickwork, ceramics and ironwork.

Guimard was also responsible for another block of apartments a little further on, where Rues Gros and Agar come into Rue La Fontaine. The design of the monochrome building, erected about fifteen years after Castel Béranger, is much more restrained. This was one of the architect's biggest undertakings. The small Guimard bar on the corner of Rue La Fontaine and Rue Gros has been preserved.

Hôtel Mezzara at 6 Rue La Fontaine, built in 1911 for a textile manufacturer, is now state property. The wrought-iron and ironwork staircase and, above all, the dining room entirely furnished by Guimard, may be seen on appointment (tel: 01.40.50.43.43).

From Passy with love

RUSSIAN-STYLE COUNTRY COTTAGES IN VILLA BEAUSÉJOUR
7 BOULEVARD BEAUSÉJOUR
Métro: La Muette

alongside what is left of the Auteuil railway line, no longer used today. Villa Beauséjour is a cul-de-sac which starts at 7 Boulevard Beauséjour, between a pale pink house and a series of small, 19th-century buildings. Adolphe Alphand, creator of so many squares and parks in Paris, had a beautiful, neoclassical residence built here, and lived in it until his death in 1891.

However, the cul-de-sac is really more well-known for its charming Russian-style country cottages at the far end (nos. 3 ter, 4 and 6). Built out of brick and stone, and covered in wood, the four houses come from the Russian stand at the 1867 World Fair. Only one of them originated from Saint Petersburg, and was sent to Paris in kit form. The other three were built by French architect Paul Bénard, according to plans drawn up by the Russians. In 1872, landowner Alphonse Lasnier bought the cottages in order to create this unusual setting, just a stone's throw from La Muette métro station.

B oulevard Beauséjour follows the route of an old avenue in the former Beauséjour park, and runs

Spring water... and wine

THE WINE MUSEUM (CAVEAU DES ÉCHANSONS)
RUE DES EAUX/5 SQUARE CHARLES-DICKENS
Open every day from 10 am to 6 pm. Tel: 01.45.25.63.26. Métro: Passy

Some steps below Passy métro station lead to the secluded Rue des Eaux. The name of the street is a reminder of the numerous chalybeate springs which used to rise here and a little further up, towards Rue Raynouard. These springs of healing water are now connected to the City of Paris water mains.

The museum – a small house several storeys high – looks lost amidst a veritable forest of tall buildings. It is devoted to wine, winemaking and the history of wine, and is the only one of its kind, because of both its site and its collection of wines. Let's push open the door... In summer, this museum is a pleasantly cool place to be in.

Inside, there are galleries which have have been dug out of the rock and converted into exhibition rooms. They used to be quarries, discovered in the fifties by a restaurant owner, who first of all made them into a wine cellar for the Eiffel Tower restaurants, and then had the excellent idea of opening it to the public.

Chaillot Hill was still covered by a vast forest – the Rouvray Forest – in the 6th century, when some monks decided to clear a few acres of ground in order to settle there. Nigeon manor house was to expand and prosper. Simply dressed in long, hooded frocks with cord girdles knotted in five places, the monks, nicknamed the "bonshommes" (good-hearted men), converted most of the hill into an enormous vineyard (the name of Rue Vineuse – literally, vine-covered street – serves as a reminder). Later, when they discovered the existence of Chaillot clay, they built a cellar, still here today, and visitors are invited to taste a glass of wine before returning to city life in the 20th century.

Paris by the seaside

CITÉ DES FLEURS
154 AVENUE DE CLICHY/59 RUE DE LA JONQUIÈRE
Métro: Brochant

A historical guide to Paris, published in 1910, affirmed that when walking down here, "you suddenly felt as if you had been transported to a quiet, attractive street in a seaside resort". This bumpy road with its pillars and cast-iron oriental vases certainly has a provincial air about it. In the mid-19th century, Mr Lhenry and Mr Bacqueville divided their land into lots, and imposed restrictive conditions on the builders – the height of the houses, three trees in the front gardens, the design of the cast-iron vases – and even stipulated the variety of flowers to be planted in the vases!

No. 17, built in 1852, has a double stairway. A monogram, "C.S.", and some oak-leaf motifs are the only embellishment on the otherwise plain façade at no. 21. No. 25, a one-storeyed building, has some cabled columns. No. 29, typical of most of the houses in this street, has a neo-Renaissance façade, an entrance topped with grotesque figures, and black and white marble inlays at first-floor level. Above the window on the left, there is a relief of a small elephant. The pink and white façade at no. 31 has two medallions. No. 33, similar in style to no. 25, is better preserved, and cabled columns ornament its picturesque façade.

A château with a road through the middle

THE FORMERLY CHÂTEAU DES TERNES, 17-9 RUE PIERRE-DEMOURS/RUE BAYEN
Métro: Ternes

"Château des Ternes" has the unusual feature of a pedestrian area – part of Rue Bayen – running through it. A portal, some relics in the grass, and two 18th-century façades are all that remains of the vast property.

15th-century plans and records show that a fortified farm existed here, surrounded by wide expanses of countryside. The domain expanded over the years, and a great deal of land was added to it. One of the owners, protégé of Richelieu, statesman and cardinal under Louis XIII and virtual ruler of France, succeeded in raising it to the status of a seigneury in 1634.

The château often changed hands, either through inheritance or sale, and was always being converted, but it was undoubtedly in the mid-18th century that it reached the height of its fame, when it became a magnificent, exquisitely furnished residence, decorated with tapestries from Flanders. The domain included a vegetable garden, an orangery, a dovecote... and afforded a beautiful view over the surrounding parkland.

However, architect Samson-Nicolas Lenoir, who became the new owner of the domain in 1778, was also a speculator. He sold all the furniture, including the park ornaments, and built a new road right through the main building (Rue Bayen). He parcelled out the parkland, and set up his own irons factory on one of the plots of land.

Swamped by city development in the 19th century, the domain became the "village" of Ternes, with a population of 8,000 in 1840.

Houses shrouded in greenery

VILLA DES TERNES
39 RUE GUERSANT/96 AVENUE DES TERNES
Métro: Porte Maillot

This "rural" residential area was created in 1822 on the site of an amusement park, a precursor, with its scenic railway, of the famous Luna Park at Porte Maillot. The owner, Mr de Verzy also created the "Panstereorama" which displayed views of major cities in Europe at the time.

Avenues des Pavillons, des Arts, du Manoir and de la Chapelle are all turnings off the area' s slightly winding main road, Avenue de Verzy, ending at Avenue des Ternes. Avenue de la Chapelle gets its name from a temporary chapel, set up for benefit of the population of the village of Ternes.

At 10 Avenue de Verzy, there is an amazing building – decorated with a bas-relief, a tribute to fine art – erected around 1910. Next door, no. 8 bis is covered entirely with glazed bricks, creating a flowing effect all the way down from the sixth floor. Opposite, no. 11 is a small country house resembling those that could be seen in the village of Ternes in the early 19th century. No. 5, built by Albert Colart in 1904, is an imposing Art Nouveau edifice, decorated under the roof with garlands.

People such as politician Paul de Cassagnac, dramatist Théodore Barrière, composer Victor Massé, and writer Edmond About took refuge in Villa des Ternes. Painter and illustrator Théophile Alexandre Steinlen, famous for his pictures of cats, also lived here. He illustrated *Chanson des Gueux* (Song of the Beggars), written by his neighbour in Rue Galvani, Jean Richepin.

Room 13

CITÉ LEMERCIER
28 RUE LEMERCIER
Métro: La Fourche or Place de Clichy

Freshly paved, Cité Lemercier looks like a humble little alley of the past. An attractive house on the left, ornamented with plaster reliefs and statuettes, is an early 19th-century "folly", now housing an artist's atelier. The gardens at nos. 1 to 7 are hidden from view by ivy, while further down at nos. 8 and 9, two brick pillars stand at the entrance. The best time to visit Rue Lemercier is when the roses are in full bloom, and their fragrance fills the entire alley.

You may encounter an old lady who will tell you about a certain Jacques Brel, Belgian-born singer and composer, famous for his song entitled *Ne me quitte pas* (If you go away), who used to live at the Chalet Hotel (no. 9) when he was young and penniless.

The singer, who was reserved and discreet, made an indelible impression on those who saw him here. The artist kept on room 13 nearly all his life, regularly paying the bill for a place he no longer came back to, but which remained close to his heart. The following words: "Jacques Brel, born on September 8th, 1929, passport no. E 083513", were written by hand in the hotel register.

A "mobile" chapel

NOTRE-DAME-DE-LA-COMPASSION CHAPEL
2 BOULEVARD AURELLE-DE-PALADINES
Métro: Porte Maillot

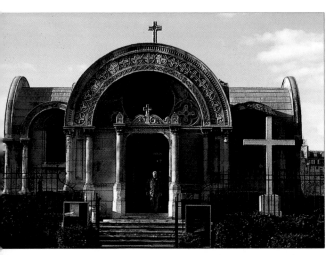

Saint-Ferdinand chapel on Place de la Porte des Ternes – not far from the roaring traffic on the nearby circular road – appears somewhat of an anachronism.

The chapel commemorates the death of Louis-Philippe's son, Duke Ferdinand d'Orléans, on July 13th, 1842, following an accident, when his carriage swerved and he was flung to the ground. The prince was immediately carried into grocer Cordier's house nearby, but to no avail. An exact replica of the room in which he died was created at Neuilly château, and fitted out with the grocer's own furniture. Cordier was given an annuity from the Civil List, and made warden at Versailles Château museum.

It was also decided that a chapel – a small, hybrid building in the form of a Greek cross – be erected on the site of the grocer's shop. It was consecrated on July 11th, 1843. Inside, the monument is a very expressive representation of the duke dying on the grocer's mattress, dressed in his army inspector general's uniform. The angel, a creation of Princess Marie, Ferdinand's sister, has been placed above the head of the deceased.

Sèvres glass factory made the fourteen stained-glass windows, based on cartoons by Ingres. Royal features can be recognized on most of the saints' faces; to the left of the altar, Louis-Philippe wearing the frock of his patron saint, Saint Louis, and on the right, Queen Marie-Aurélie's long face. Christ's face is represented by that of Ferdinand d'Orléans, the deceased.

When alterations were made at Porte Maillot in 1970, the chapel was dismantled and reassembled, stone by stone, and moved 150 metres further along.

A château for the Bank of France

HÔTEL GAILLARD
1 PLACE DU GÉNÉRAL-CATROUX
Métro: Malesherbes

H ôtel Gaillard, prestige branch office of the Bank of France, has a certain elegance. Its architect, Jules Février, drew his inspiration from a wing of Blois château to build this manor house for the Manager of the Bank of France, Émile Gaillard. Building work was completed in 1844, and the house was decorated with

original, 16th-century wainscotting and sculptures, and fitted out with magnificent furniture from Issogne château in the Aoste valley. The banker's vast art collection included a Murillo portraying Saint Anthony of Padua, a portrait of Henry II, King of France and husband of Catherine de Médicis, along with some fine, 17th-century Flemish works. A sumptuous, costumed ball, to which 2,000 people were invited, was held on April 11th, 1885 to inaugurate the building.

The banker died on May 5th, 1904, and his valuable collections were rapidly broken up. It was not until 1919 that a new owner – the Bank of France – was found for the

manor house, whose character was not affected by the alterations that had to be made. For instance, the basement was used as a safe-deposit room, protected by a ditch full of water. This original safety device gave rise to a fantastic rumour according to which crocodiles were let out at night to better protect the valuables deposited in the safes!

The façade overlooking the street looks particularly opulent. The letter "G" appears on the dormers in the roof, and there are grotesque figures above the small entrance; the one carrying the purse looks like banker Gaillard, and the other, holding a square, resembles architect Février.

155

Misty alley

CHÂTEAU OF THE MIST
ALLÉE DES BROUILLARDS (RUE GIRARDON)
Métro: Lamarck-Caulaincourt

The romantic Allée des Brouillards – a narrow street off Place des Quatre-Frères-Casadessus, giving access to Rue Girardon – is the focal point of the history of Montmartre. On the right-hand side, at the far end of a lawn, stands the delightful façade of the famous "Château des Brouillards" (Château of the Mist), in front of which countless artists have set up their easels.

In the 17th century, a small farm and a mill used to stand here, shrouded in mist on stormy days, hence the name. In 1764, a large, walled piece of land, including the dilapidated farmhouse and mill, was sold to a high judicial court advocate, who ordered the building of a fine residence, the "Maison des Brouillards" (House of the Mist). It used to be a pleasant country house complete with farmyard, orchard, cellars and wells.

After a visit to this romantic château, poet Gerard de Nerval described it as "such a light structure! A small house in the style of Pompeii, something like the house of the ill-fated poet". In 1850, after the outbuildings were demolished to make way for some small houses, one of which was occupied by painter Renoir, the château and its surroundings deteriorated considerably. Tramps and delinquents invaded the house, and shabby-looking shacks gradually encroached on its parkland, which eventually became the famous "maquis", so dear to the hearts of nostalgic Montmartre locals.

It was twenty years before the owner of the château – a fine name for what was not much more than a ruin – began to restore it, and took steps towards preserving it. In fact, at one point, the City of Paris was planning to do away with the alley and demolish the old house in order to establish a link between Rue Girardon and Rue Simon-Dereure. Fortunately, the "Château of the Mist" was saved from demolition, and is visited every year by people in love with Montmartre and in search of its rural, picturesque past.

The dear old maquis

MONTMARTRE "MAQUIS"
65 RUE LEPIC
Métro: Abbesses

An inconspicuous entrance at 65 Rue Lepic gives access to a steep stairway. The passage, which has never been given a name, leads to what remains of the Montmartre "maquis". Halfway down, there is a platform bearing an enormous rock, fragment of some rockery garden. An abandoned house on the right emphasizes the romantic air of the place. Just before this picturesque little alley comes into Avenue Junot, there is a piece of land on the right, where there is always a game of bowls going on. This is the last part of the maquis, which, but for the perseverance of the local residents who put up a fierce fight a few years ago to save the place from the hands

of a property developer who wanted to build a car park, would have disappeared altogether.

Before the lovely Avenue Junot was built in 1909, this used to be an immense wasteland, the famous maquis (see pp. 156-57). It was dotted with miserable shacks full of penniless daubers and destitute Montmartre locals, whose presence there was undoubtedly one of the reasons why the picture of the good-natured tramp – a "quaint" Montmartre souvenir –, became so popular.

At the end of the passage, turn left into Avenue Junot and go along to no. 23 where there is a delightful cul-de-sac, Villa Léandre, whose brick houses look very British in style.

Left: Montmartre maquis, paradise for bowls' players.
Above: The attractive Villa Léandre.

"Château Montmartre"

MONTMARTRE VINEYARDS
RUE SAINT-VINCENT AND RUE DES SAULES
Métro: Lamarck-Caulaincourt

On the first Saturday in October, Montmartre locals pay a thundering tribute to Bacchus during a symbolic celebration of the Rue Saint-Vincent wine harvest. There is a 17th-century saying which explains in explicit terms how Montmartre wine acts as a diuretic, one quart producing four!

The two thousand, four hundred Montmartre vines, planted in terraced rows on five levels, yield a rather vinegarish wine, which, in all honesty, cannot be classified among the best vintages. This former wasteland was converted into a public garden, and later into vineyards, at the instigation of painter Poulbot, who was determined not to let the land fall into the hands of a property developer. The first wine harvest in October 1934 was not very good, and it was not until the seventies that the vines – Gamay and Pinot noir – were better tended, and yielded a more palatable juice.

The harvested grapes are collected and pressed in the basement of the 18th arrondissement city hall, and the juice is stored in large barrels to ferment. Every year, around 700 bottles, labelled "Clos Montmartre", are brought out of the cellars and sold to raise funds for the 18th arrondissement Festival Committee.

Whose street is this?

CITÉ VÉRON
94 BOULEVARD DE CLICHY
Métro: Blanche

A blue and white enamel sign announces a long cul-de-sac, next door to the Moulin-Rouge, threading its way between the buildings. Though the alley's measurements may be modest (80 x 3 metres), its residents were held in high esteem, with the exception, however, of those who lived there before World War II, when Cité Véron was a haunt for delinquents from seedy Pigalle with its nightclubs and its prostitutes' hotels.

In 1953, poet Jacques Prévert moved into no. 6 bis Cité Véron, where he lived for twenty years. Writer Boris Vian, who also spent much of his time playing jazz, lived in the apartment opposite, where, surrounded by a few books and very little furniture, he wrote *L'Arrache-Cœur* (Heartsnatcher) and many of his songs, including *Le Déserteur* (The Deserter) for which he was also famous. Writer Raymond Queneau, dramatist Ionesco, and many others used to meet on the communal terrace, site of the French cancan dancers' dressing rooms in the early 20th century.

Life in the cul-de-sac was recently disrupted by the arrondissement council's decision to rename the street after humorist Pierre Dac. This was not all to the liking of the residents, particularly Prévert's and Vian's descendants, who pointed out that Pierre Dac had never set foot in the place! After the usual preliminary excitement, vigorous protests, and a search for influential support, this delightful cul-de-sac in the heart of old Pigalle officially retrieved its former name.

Incidentally, who was Véron? A local resident, mayor of Montmartre from 1830 to 1841, and an honest citizen, who certainly never imagined that his name would continue to be so heroicly defended at the end of the 20th century!

Nutmeg, vanilla and theology...

7 IMPASSE MARIE-BLANCHE
Métro: Blanche

The attractive, medieval-looking building in Impasse Marie-Blanche is an unusual sight. It belonged to antique dealer Eymonaud, and provides us with an excuse for mentioning the house that Count Charles de l'Escalopier had built in Rue Joseph-de-Maistre nearby in 1835. The 1837 yearbook on the surroundings of Paris contains a glowing description of this very strange house, characteristic of its owner's tastes. It had steam-heated greenhouses decorated with rocks and pools, and was open to the public. Exotic trees, particularly banana trees, were the main attraction, not to mention sandalwood, nutmeg, coconut, vanilla, mangosteen and copaiba trees.

In 1840, Count de l'Escalopier applied for and obtained the post of librarian at the Arsenal Library (public library in the 4th arrondissement). He subsequently devoted himself entirely to his passion for research, and razed the greenhouses to make way for a library containing around 6,000 volumes, of which nearly 2,000 were works on theology!

A small museum devoted entirely to the Middle Ages adjoined the library. Charles de l'Escalopier, an eccentric typical of the last century (reminiscent of Bouvard and Pécuchet, characters in an unfinished, satirical work by Flaubert who criticized amateurish dabbling in science), died in Liancourt in 1861. The charming, Gothic Revival castle was demolished in 1882, but you can still see some of its relics, sculptures in particular, on the façade of the beautiful, elaborately yet delicately structured house in Impasse Marie-Blanche, but don't expect to find any bananas!

The oldest house in Montmartre

MONTMARTRE MUSEUM
12 RUE CORTOT
Open every day except Mondays from 11 am to 6 pm. Tel: 01.46.01.61.11. Métro: Lamarck-Caulaincourt

Montmartre museum has found shelter in the oldest house in Montmartre, at the top of the hill. The house escaped demolition thanks to architect Claude Charpentier, and restoration work began in 1958. Beyond the small shop overlooking Rue Cortot, a tree-lined road leads up to the entrance of the museum, a living shrine to the history of Montmartre.

Located on the hillside, this pretty white house was bought by Claude de la Rose, known as both Rosimond and Jean-Baptiste Dumesnil, in 1680. He was an actor in Molière's troup, and, like the playwright, died on stage during a performance of *Le Malade imaginaire* (The Imaginary Invalid).

In the 19th century, many artists lived and worked in the old house on Rue Cortot. In 1875, Auguste Renoir, in search of an atelier near the Moulin de la Galette, moved into two rooms under the roof and a lean-to on the ground floor. It was here that he painted some of his most famous paintings, such as *The Swing* or *Dance at the Moulin de la Galette.* Suzanne Valadon and her son, Maurice Utrillo, lived in the atelier, annexe to the museum, on the second floor on the Rue Cortot side of the building. Here, amid quarrels, broken dishes, and tears, Utrillo found the energy to paint when he was not under the influence of alcohol. Sketch artist Poulbot, painter Raoul Dufy, painter and engraver Démitrius Galanis, actor and theatre director Antoine, and poet Pierre Reverdy were also occupants of the house on Rue Cortot.

Here, the fine collections of the Historical Society for Old Montmartre have found the home they deserve. Temporary exhibitions are held regularly, whereas some superb pieces of Clignancourt porcelain, together with historical reconstructions such as musician Gustave Charpentier's study, are permanently on view.

From the museum windows, there is an exceptionally beautiful view of the gardens and the vineyard, and, further down in the distance, of Paris shrouded in mist.

Stairway C

VILLA DES ARTS
15 RUE HÉGÉSIPPE-MOREAU
Métro: Place de Clichy

was responsible for its elegant buildings. He salvaged building materials to first of all erect the houses lining the courtyard. The amazing stairway on the right is said to have come from a pavilion built for the 1900 World Fair. Opposite the cemetery in Rue Ganneron, an ingenious cascading structure comprising about sixty ateliers provides artists with excellent lighting conditions.

There was a continuous flow of celebrities through the doors of these ateliers, including, between 1899 and 1901, Eugène Carrière, Paul Signac, and Paul Cézanne who painted his famous portrait of gallery owner Ambroise Vollard, which required more than a hundred sittings! Louis Marcoussis, Jean and Raoul Dufy also contributed to the renown of the place. It was here that Nicolas Schöffer created his very first cybernetic sculpture and a spatio-, luminodynamic work, still exhibited in his atelier which is now a private museum.

This charming area, so characteristic of the atmosphere of 19th-century Montmartre with its artists' ateliers, has often been used as a film set, for instance by Fellini for *The Clowns*, and by Jean-Charles Tacchella for *Escalier C* (Stairway C).

Access to Villa des Arts is through a fine wrought-iron gate, and the name of the street is cut out in the curved metal arc above the entrance.

When Desmichel and Gueret decided to restructure the entire block in 1888, this cul-de-sac was already in existence; Henri Cambon

Mother Nature in Paris

SAINT-VINCENT NATURE GARDEN (OPPOSITE 14 RUE SAINT-VINCENT)
Open to the public from April to October on Mondays from 4 to 6 pm (except during school holidays) and Saturdays from 2 to 6 pm. Tel: 01.43.28.47.63. (Paris-Nature Department). Métro: Lamarck-Caulaincourt

© Paris-Nature

Overlooking Rue Saint-Vincent, the nature garden is all that remains of the forest of Montmartre. This little enclosure was laid out in 1985 by the City of Paris Parks and Gardens Department, who periodically opens the garden to the public, while making sure it retains its natural state. In order to recreate an area of natural parkland on a small scale, the Department had to consolidate the sloping land, lay out a path, and dig a pool.

This garden really is just as Mother Nature created it: not one tree nor bush has been planted by a gardener. The vegetation runs wild, and is untouched by human hand, except when it becomes necessary to protect it from the city environment. Annuals and plants, which cannot grow in the shade, or are unable to survive competition, gradually give way to the more resistant, woody or perennial species.

A large number of insects, small animals and birds find shelter in this miniature forest, and are barely disturbed by the garden's rare visitors. Since 1988, only conducted tours – veritable lessons in practical ecology right in the middle of Paris – are allowed, and are by appointment only. Schoolchildren, and the general public, can come and stroll in this nature garden, and learn how to respect the environment.

Artists' quarters

"MONTMARTRE AUX ARTISTES"
187-93 RUE ORDENER
Métro: Jules-Joffrin

Inside the beautiful brick building, a big entrance hall, whose walls are covered with brightly coloured ceramics, leads to a complex of artists' ateliers. Sculptor Louis-Aimé Lejeune, along with a few friends, created a real-estate company, whose main objective was to provide decent accommodation for artists. At that time, the availability of housing of this nature was not sufficient to meet the enormous demand.

Adolphe Thiers drew the plans of the future complex, which was built in 1930. It comprises three buildings containing 187 ateliers with very big windows, all facing north. There was something very attractive about the atmosphere in the courtyards, despite the plainness of the white walls dotted with rusty balconies. This was undoubtedly due to that special feeling of living on the outskirts of the city, while nevertheless remaining in close contact with it.

Adolphe Thiers accomplished a great deal in Montmartre, notably the ateliers at 36 Avenue Junot (very similar in layout to those in Rue Ordener), a house at 22 Rue Simon-Dereure, and two hotels at 24 and 26 Avenue Junot.

Swimming pool or cinema?

PUBLIC SWIMMING POOL
13 RUE DES AMIRAUX
Métro: Simplon

What street could be more aptly named than Rue des Amiraux (Admirals' Street), where an imposing, white-tiled building, built by Henri Sauvage (1922-7), stands like some majestic liner lying at anchor?

Built for the City of Paris, and originally intended as low-income housing, the structure is based on criteria already adopted by the architect at 26 Rue Vavin in the 6th arrondissement. The apartments are tiered, have terraces, and are extremely light. The outside walls are covered entirely with white tiles like those you see in the métro.

The main issue concerned the decision on how the building's interior space, created by the unusual, tiered layout of its structure, could be usefully employed. Sauvage thought of installing a cinema, whereas the City of Paris wanted a swimming pool. Those who control the purse strings generally win... and the swimming pool is still open today.

Stolen roses

SAINT-VINCENT CEMETERY, 6 RUE LUCIEN-GAULARD
Open Mondays to Fridays, 8 am to 5.30 pm, Saturdays, 8.30 am to 5.30 pm, Sundays 9 am to 5.30 pm.
Métro: Lamarck-Caulaincourt

Saint-Vincent Cemetery, dominated by the Sacré-Cœur.

In addition to the cemetery in Avenue Rachel, Montmartre has another two lesser known, but nevertheless very interesting, graveyards. The first, Calvaire Cemetery, adjoining Saint-Pierre de Montmartre Church, is open on All Saints' Day only, whereas the second, the little Saint-Vincent Cemetery, is much more accessible, and affords a superb view of the "Lapin Agile" cabaret, the vineyard, Montmartre Museum and, of course, the dome of the Sacré-Cœur, which you cannot fail to notice.

This modest enclosure is the final resting place – a kind of promised land – for the souls of Montmartre locals, after a life of sadness or happiness, more or less in the public eye. You will find the names of well-known Montmartre families, after whom streets have been named – Tourlaque, Labat, Muller, Lavigne, etc. A large number of celebrities are buried here: Émile Goudeau, founder and president of the Society of Hydropathy, writer Marcel Aymé, cabaret singer Gabriello, painters Maurice Utrillo, Gen Paul, Jules Adler, Eugène Boudin, actor Harry Baur, musicians Arthur Honnegger and Désiré Inghelbrecht. Théophile Alexandre Steinlen, author of eloquent depictions of cats and human suffering, was laid to rest under a tree in the south-east corner of the cemetery.

Roland Dorgelès, a fine writer who became strongly attached to Montmartre, is also buried here. "Often," he wrote, "when a friend couldn't afford to buy a bunch of flowers for his girlfriend on her name day, he would slip into the old cemetery and filch a few roses from the flowers of a recent funeral." Those no longer in the land of the living could not really begrudge him this, since Montmartre, as everybody knows, is a favourite haunt for lovers.

An air of Russia

SAINT-SERGE CHURCH
93 RUE DE CRIMÉE
Métro: Laumière

A path – where an old vine creeps up the walls – leads to a small, colourful house, decorated with a fresco representing Saint Serge de Radogène. Turn right, and walk past some apartment buildings and a dilapidated wooden construction – formerly a Protestant dispensary and now a workshop for making church candles – until you see, at the top of some steps, Saint-Serge Church with its amazing wooden porch.

Built in 1861, this chapel was Protestant with an active congregation of Prussian immigrants until 1914, when it became Orthodox. The property belonged to the Germans, was requisitioned after World War I, and then sold by auction. In 1924, the Orthodox Church announced their intention of buying it on July 18th, Saint Serge's day according to the Julian calendar. The inflow of Russian emigrants fleeing the October Revolution made it necessary to open a new religious centre.

Between 1925 and 1927, Dimitri S. Stelletsky supervised the decoration work. The wooden porch and the outside stairway were built on in 1925. Some representations of the defenders of the Orthodox faith before Russia was converted can be seen on the walls alongside the stairs leading into the church on the first floor.

The interior is splendid. Scenes from the Old Testament can be seen on the walls of the narthex: Noah's Ark, the Burning Bush, and the three adolescent boys in the blazing fire. Pictures of twelve saints, symbolizing Orthodox feast days, are painted on the walls of the nave. On the icon wall at the far end, Christ in majesty is represented, surrounded by the animal symbols of the Evangelists.

A paradise for little boys

THE FORMER MECCANO FACTORY
78-80 RUE RÉBEVAL
Métro: Pyrénées

Rue Rébeval was once a country road leading to the Saint-Laurent district via Chemin de la Chopinette. In order to get the best view of this street, start at the Rue de Belleville end, and slowly walk down towards Boulevard de la Villette.

Before it became what is now the Paris-Belleville School of Architecture, the building on the left-hand side at nos. 78-80, with its extraordinary rounded, brick and freestone façade, used to house the Meccano factory workshops. Millions of little pieces of metal which inspired generations of budding mechanics were manufactured here.

In former times, Rue Rébeval had lots of small side streets giving access to Chaumont hill with its quarries and windmills. Cité Jandelle, which turns off at 55 Rue Rébeval, no doubt follows the track of one of those country paths. The cul-de-sac itself is not very inviting; however, at the far end there are some old Belleville country houses, surrounded by greenery, which have been restored and painted in bright colours.

"Industrial Venice"

THE FORMER "MAGASINS GÉNÉRAUX DE PARIS" WAREHOUSES
QUAI DE LA GIRONDE
Métro: Corentin-Cariou

Industrial buildings converted into housing and offices.

and unload their precious cargo before leaving for Aubervilliers port. A wet dock enabled bargemen to enter the Magasins Généraux de Paris warehouses, known as "Industrial Venice". The former industrial activity of the warehouses, which stretch over an area of 12,000 square metres, has now ceased. The buildings were stripped and restored about fifteen years ago to house offices and apartments. However, the expected activity failed to materialize, leaving the warehouses looking somewhat deserted.

They can be seen lining the canal near a small square. The excellent view – from the bridge over the canal – of the buildings standing in water, linked by a delightful footbridge, is marred by a temporary fence. Hopefully, things will liven up in the district, and make it a pleasant place to take a stroll in.

I n the old days, after leaving the Villette slaughterhouses, a great many barges used to come down Saint-Denis canal to Quai de la Gironde (thus named since 1863),

Such a pretty village…

RUES ÉMILE-DESVAUX AND PAUL-DE-KOCK
Métro: Télégraphe

Located between Rue des Bois and Rue de Romainville, a small, attractive group of houses and small apartment buildings in Rue Émile-Desvaux and Rue Paul-de-Kock, dating back to the thirties and reminiscent of the "Mouzaïa" area nearby (see pp. 174-75), can be seen at the top of a slope.

The roads form a loop and are lined with imaginatively-built houses, which make the area look like a picturesque village in the middle of the 19th arrondissement. It is difficult to say which house is the most beautiful and the most original. An ancient pediment, a mosaic frieze, an attractively-designed window, a sweet-smelling rose tree, or even a roof terrace as in the case of Villa Koutok at 17 Rue Émile-Desvaux – each house has something to enchant visitors coming to this little "village" on the outskirts of the city.

A quiet life in the city

11 AND 13 RUE DES FÊTES
Métro: Place des Fêtes

Rue des Fêtes used to be the road to Belleville village fairs, hence its name. At no. 11, *mascarons* have been stuck on the façade of the one-storeyed manor house with a pointed roof in an apparent effort to differentiate it from an ordinary suburban type of house. This enormous building dates back to 1882, and is an example of the pretentious style sometimes adopted by architects at that time.

Next door, at no. 13, behind an iron gate, a shady, mysterious path leads to a charming group of houses, built on the former garden of the manor house in 1906. On either side of a small path, modest-looking houses nestle in the surrounding greenery.

The atmosphere here is relaxed. There is a tall chestnut tree and some lilac trees in the tiny gardens, providing shade for children at play; adventurous cats are free to roam; and the local residents quietly get on with their lives. A small, unusual, wooden summerhouse adds to the bucolic charm of the place, which appears quite cut off from the city.

"Quarries of America"

THE MOUZAÏA DISTRICT
AREA SURROUNDING RUE DE LA MOUZAÏA AND RUE MIGUEL-HIDALGO
Métro: Danube

Above: Villa Rimbaud.
Opposite: Villa Claude-Monet.

The picturesque area around Rue Miguel-Hidalgo and Rue de la Mouzaïa, between Buttes-Chaumont Park and Square de la Butte-du-Chapeau-Rouge, makes a welcome change of scenery. You can feel the atmosphere of the place as soon as you come out of Danube métro station. Here, there are no high-rises, just buildings with one or two storeys at the most. It looks as if a quiet corner of suburbia has been transplanted to the city. The light structure of the buildings is explained by the nature of the substratum: gypsum was quarried here from the Middle Ages right up to the 19th century.

The plaster of Paris obtained by partly dehydrating the gypsum was exported to places as far away as Louisiana during the last century; most of Rue Manin used to be known as the street of the "Quarries of America".

When quarrying stopped in 1872, the unstable state of the subsoil was not considered suitable for the reconstruction of the district of "America". There were very few people willing to build on land riddled with holes; the presence of a few shacks on barren mounds of earth was as far as city planning went in those days. However, it did become an excellent base for dropouts, pickpockets and criminals of all kinds.

When the entrances to the quarries were filled in, housing developments began very gradually to take shape along the main roads of the area, where people risked building small, brick or stone houses, fronted by tiny gardens full of rambling roses and ivy. They provided modest, but convenient, lodgings for factory workers on the east side of Paris. Life was good in the countryside around

Paris, not far from Belleville and near Buttes-Chaumont. Today, the population has changed; most of the local residents today quite obviously do not work shifts!

Wandering along these side streets produces an indefinable feeling of contentment. The simply built, colourful little houses, tucked away behind fences, are a captivating, cheerful sight, and, in spring, the fruit trees and flowers scent the air everywhere. No longer known as the "Quarries of America", the area gets its name – Mouzaïa – from a locality in Algeria.

Above: Rue Rémy-de-Gourmont.
Opposite: Rue Edgar-Poë.

A view over Paris

BUTTE BERGEYRE

RUES GEORGES-LARDENNOIS, RÉMY-DE-GOURMONT, EDGAR-POË, PHILIPPE-HECHT
Métro: Bolivar

Before World War I, there used to be an amusement park with merry-go-rounds and sideshows on the spot where Rue Georges-Lardennois begins. "Les Folles Buttes", the name of the fair, is no longer there, but Butte Bergeyre (Bergeyre Hill) with its attractive houses built in the twenties and thirties is still flourishing.

The most charming feature of this unusual site, wedged between Avenue Simon-Bolivar and Avenue Mathurin-Moreau, is its atmosphere of a timeless, sleepy village in the country a long way out of the city, or perhaps it would be more accurate to say, a long way above the city, as anyone who has climbed the steps in Rue Barrelet-de-Ricou or clambered up winding Rue Georges-Lardennois will confirm! The character of the place certainly stems from its high altitude, and if you stand at the junction of Rue Georges-Lardennois and Rue Rémy-de-Gourmont, you will find yourself looking out over a beautiful panorama of the city of Paris, including an unusual view of the Sacré-Cœur.

Before coming down to earth in the busy avenues on either side, linger a while up here on the hill, and take a leisurely stroll along the tiny streets.

Flowers and bloodshed

VILLA DU BORRÉGO AND VILLA DES OTAGES
33 RUE DU BORRÉGO AND 85 RUE HAXO
Métro: Saint-Fargeau

Life is very quiet in the very attractive Villa Borrégo with its neat rows of small houses, fronted by pretty gardens. However, this was not always the case in the cul-de-sacs around Saint-Fargeau. During the Paris Commune, Villa des Otages (Hostages), which starts at 85 Rue Haxo, was the scene of a bloody incident.

A Federate colonel, Émile Goix, had about fifty prisoners – priests, soldiers, civilians – transferred there from the Roquette Prison on May 26th, 1871. Despite efforts by writer Jules Vallès and Eugène Varlin, secretary of the French section of the first International, to calm people down, an angry mob massacred the fifty hostages as well as a Federate and an onlooker who tried to stand up for the unfortunate victims. An inscription in iron lettering honours the memory of the 52 victims.

Spick and span Belleville houses

VILLA CASTEL
16 RUE DU TRANSVAAL
Métro: Couronnes

P rotected from the street by an iron gate, not always padlocked, Villa Castel comprises about ten small, spick and span, red-brick houses fitted with old-fashioned awnings. This attractive, though modest group of buildings, erected in the late 19th century, has managed to survive in a part of Belleville where property developers are not in the habit of exercising restraint when putting their excavators to work. Unfortunately, the cul-de-sacs along Rue des Envierges or Rue Piat have not been quite so lucky.

An impostor and a drinker

CHARONNE CEMETERY
111 RUE DE BAGNOLET
Métro: Gambetta

The charming Saint-Germain-de-Charonne Church is the only church in Paris with an adjoining cemetery (except for Calvaire Cemetery in Montmartre: see p. 168). The small, country-like graveyard contains more than 650 tombs. The sons – killed in a car accident – of writer André Malraux are buried here, as is writer Robert Brasillach, sentenced to death and executed at the time of the Liberation in 1945. The latter wrote this about the cemetery: "[I love] this place where only trees and a country church tower are to be seen, and where the huge city with its tall buildings is lost from view."

At the far, left-hand side of the cemetery, a bronze statue of a dignified old man, wearing a cocked hat, stands on top of the tomb of a certain François-Éloy Bègue, known as "old Malgloire", and who liked to pass himself off as secretary to French revolutionary Robespierre. The truth of the matter was less spectacular: he was a house painter (1750-1838), enjoyed life, and drank a good deal. Legend has it that he was buried with a bottle of wine.

The statue has nothing to do with the deceased, since it was Malgloire's friend and landlord, Mr Herbeaumont, a scrap metal merchant by profession, who unearthed it from some junkyard or other and put it on his tomb.

Once outside the cemetery, you will be able to savour the convivial atmosphere, often reminiscent of life in a village, of the streets in the Saint-Blaise district.

Grand châteaus in the 20th arrondissement

PAVILLON DE L'ERMITAGE, 148 RUE DE BAGNOLET
Métro: Porte de Bagnolet

When Belleville was surrounded by countryside, the aristocracy and wealthy Parisians found it most attractive. There were rich country houses everywhere, not to mention sizeable estates. However, the end of the 18th century proved fatal to most grand châteaus. Nothing remains of Château de Charonne, where cardinal Richelieu liked to stay, nor of

Château de Bruyères, which belonged to Prince de Rohan. The same goes for the biggest château of all, Château de Ménilmontant, which extended over an area whose boundaries would have run along Rue de Romainville, Rue Pelleport, Rue du Surmelin, and out to Boulevard Mortier.

Built in 1734, Pavillon de l'Ermitage escaped demolition and is all that remains of Château de Bagnolet, which used to belong to the Duchess of Orleans. The surface area of the estate is difficult to imagine today – eighty hectares comprising trees, thickets, and gardens with long avenues. A path, Allée de Madame, later to become Rue des Orteaux, was laid out in order to avoid the congestion in Rue de Bagnolet when

coming to the estate. The splendours of this way of life did not last, and in 1769 the property was parcelled out, deforested and sold by lots. In 1787, Baron de Batz-Lomagne bought the Pavillon de l'Ermitage for 36,000 pounds of silver. His residence soon became the headquarters for counter-revolutionaries, who attempted to save Louis XVI from his tragic fate (he was guillotined in 1793). On June 17th, 1794, the fifty-four "Charonne conspirators" were guillotined on Place du Trône. Their leader was nowhere to be found... but was later awarded the Order of Saint Louis in 1823.

You will appreciate the subtle quality of rear façade of the pavilion from the Debrousse public garden.

"La Campagne à Paris"

RUE JULES-SIEGFRIED, RUE IRÉNÉE-BLANC (AND SURROUNDING AREA)
Métro: Porte de Bagnolet

Several flights of steps lead up to the attractive housing development, "La Campagne à Paris" (Country in Paris), perched high up, almost a hundred metres, above Porte de Bagnolet métro station nearby.

A leisurely walk down Rues Irénée-Blanc and Jules-Siegfried will give you a chance to examine the 89 one-storeyed houses lining these twisting, village-like streets. Built in brick or buhrstone, the neat little houses, fronted by tiny yards full of greenery and graced with small back gardens, are very much sought after by Parisians. Many of the residents are descendants of the founders of the development. Back in 1906, buying this wasteland, and building a small,

low-income housing development on it, must have been a matter of trusting to luck. Some people had such faith in the project that they founded the Campagne à Paris Company, and bought 15,800 square metres of land that nobody wanted. The substratum was unstable – a former gypsum quarry – and had been hastily filled in with rubble recuperated from the building of Avenues Gambetta and de la République. Despite this, eight shareholders began building their houses, and, in 1913, thirty-eight others followed suit. The development was finally inaugurated on June 20th, 1926, and the founders were congratulated for their tenacity.

*Left: **Rue Paul-Strauss.***
*Above: **Rue Irénée-Blanc.***

Belleville water

SAINT-MARTIN WATER INSPECTION CHAMBER
42 RUE DES CASCADES
Métro: Jourdain
Other chambers: La Lanterne (213 Rue de Belleville), Messiers (17 Rue des Cascades),
Roquette (36-8 Rue de la Mare).

The street names in the 19th and 20th arrondissements – Rues des Rigoles, de la Mare, de la Duée, des Cascades (rivulets, pond, spring, waterfalls) – recall the countless springs that used to gush forth in Belleville and its neighbouring areas. As early as the 12th century, water "from the North" was collected for religious communities such as the Saint-Lazare Hospitallers and the Saint-Martin-des-Champs Priory on the right bank. Belleville watercourses were easy to drain, and, over the centuries, were exploited to meet the constantly increasing demand for water in Paris. First of all, the water was directed along open channels, and then collected in dry-stone conduits, covered with slabs of stone and clay, leading to small inspection chambers, some of which can still be seen in the 20th arrondissement.

Near Place des Fêtes, in the 19th arrondissement, stands the handsome Lanterne chamber which used to be connected to a solid-looking aqueduct, of which there are only a very few remains today. This chamber – 4.70 metres wide and 8.80 metres high – is the biggest one of its kind still standing today. It was built between 1583 and 1613, and has an elegant dome with a lantern.

Another two inspection chambers of the Belleville aqueduct are still standing. At 17 Rue des Cascades, there is the Messiers chamber, whose name meaning "official crop watchers" recalls the occupation of rural policemen employed under the

Left: Saint-Martin chamber at 42 Rue des Cascades.
Above: Messiers chamber at no. 17 has been preserved in modern surroudings.

Ancien Régime to supervise the harvesting. The Roquette chamber (38 Rue de la Mare) mainly supplied the Roquette Convent.

A large spring under Rue de Savies used to gush forth on a piece of steeply-sloping land belonging to Saint-Martin-des-Champs Abbey. It was drained, covered, and the water collected in the Saint-Martin chamber in Rue de Savies, which turns off at 42 Rue des Cascades. Built in 1804, this stone building has two drains for the water still flowing from the embankment behind it. As early as the 13th century, pipes carried water from here to the Temple and Saint-Martin-des-Champs. Saint-Martin water was also supplied to Hôtel Saint-Pol, the residence of the future King Charles V in the heart of the Marais. (For more information on Paris water supplies, see pp. 122-3).

Contents

If you wish to know more about each individual arrondissement of Paris, and you have a good command of the French language, this is the collection for you. In every volume you will find a chapter on the history of the district concerned, together with advice on the best itineraries. In addition to renowned monuments and museums, you will also discover details on lesser-known places. These will help you to understand how Paris is still in many ways like the village it used to be, with its medieval alleys, markets stalls in the streets, and 17th-century manor houses lovingly restored by their lucky owners... Rich rewards await those who know how to seek out the essence of Paris!

180 TO 276 PAGES. 95 FF.

Denis Michel
Dominique Renou

LE
GUIDE
DU
PROMENEUR

11e
arrondissement

Faubourg Saint-Antoine
La Roquette
Richard-Lenoir
Folie-Méricourt

Parigramme

Danielle Chadych

LE
GUIDE
DU
PROMENEUR

12e
arrondissement

Picpus
Charenton
Faubourg Saint-Antoine
Bercy
Bois de Vincennes

Parigramme

Gilles-Antoine Langlois

LE
GUIDE
DU
PROMENEUR

13e
arrondissement

La Salpêtrière
Maison Blanche
La Gare
Croulebarbe

Parigramme

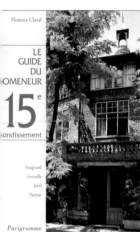

Florence Claval

LE
GUIDE
DU
PROMENEUR

15e
arrondissement

Vaugirard
Grenelle
Javel
Pasteur

Parigramme

Marie-Laure
Crosnier Leconte

LE
GUIDE
DU
PROMENEUR

16e
arrondissement

Chaillot
Passy/La Muette
Auteuil
Porte Dauphine
Bois de Boulogne

Parigramme

Rodolphe Trouilleux

LE
GUIDE
DU
PROMENEUR

17e
arrondissement

Épinettes
Batignolles
Ternes
Monceau

Parigramme

Élisabeth Philipp

LE
GUIDE
DU
PROMENEUR

19e
arrondissement

La Villette
Belleville
Les Buttes-Chaumont
Flandre

Parigramme

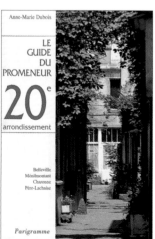

Anne-Marie Dubois

LE
GUIDE
DU
PROMENEUR

20e
arrondissement

Belleville
Ménilmontant
Charonne
Père-Lachaise

Parigramme

Conception graphique et réalisation
Fabienne Vaslet

Jacques Lebar, photographe
46, rue Voltaire, 92250 La Garenne-Colombes. France
Tel: 01.47.86.32.03. Fax: 01.47.60.10.14

Photogravure Euresys, à Baisieux
Flashage Leyre, à Paris
ISBN : 2-84096-078-8
Dépôt légal : avril 1997
Achevé d'imprimer en avril 1997
sur les presses de l'imprimerie Mame, à Tours